About this book

Symbols are used to denote the following categories:

- map reference
- address or location
- telephone number
- opening times
- admission charge
- restaurant or café on premises or nearby
- nearest underground train station
- nearest bus/tram route
- nearest overground train station
- nearest ferry stop
- other places of interest nearby
- tourist information
- other practical information
- ➤ indicates the page where you will find a fuller description

This book is divided into four sections.

Contents

Planning

RECORDI

Before You Go

WHEN TO GO

JAN	FEB	MAR	APR	MAY	JUN	JUL	AUG	SEP	OCT	NOV	DEC
16°C	17°C	18°C	21°C	23°C	27°C	29°C	29°C	27°C	23°C	19°C	17°C
61°F	63°F	64°F	70°F	73°F	81°F	84°F	84°F	81°F	73°F	66°F	63°F

High season Low season

Temperatures are the **average daily maximum** for each month. Easter is usually bright and sunny without being too hot; however, accommodation is heavily booked up. The best time to visit is in May and early June when there is plenty of sunshine and the average daytime temperature is 23°C (73°F) to 25°C (77°F). Visitor levels are not too high and there is a choice of where to stay. Peak tourist times are in July and August, when the weather is hottest. Most of the country is on holiday in August and there is a huge exodus to the coast. September and October can be delightful with sunny weather lingering well into autumn. Winters on the coast and in low-lying regions are pleasant but in the mountains expect chilly weather.

WHAT YOU NEED

● Required
○ Suggested
▲ Not required

Some countries require a passport to remain valid for a minimum period (usually at least six months) beyond the date of entry – contact their consulate or embassy or your travel agent for details.

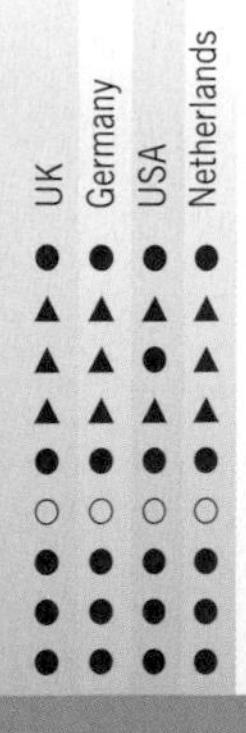

	UK	Germany	USA	Netherlands
Passport (or National Identity Card where applicable)	●	●	●	●
Visa (regulations can change – check before you travel)	▲	▲	▲	▲
Onward or Return Ticket	▲	▲	●	▲
Health Inoculations (tetanus and polio)	▲	▲	▲	▲
Health Documentation (➤ 9, Health Advice)	●	●	●	●
Travel Insurance	○	○	○	○
Driving Licence (national)	●	●	●	●
Car Insurance Certificate	●	●	●	●
Car Registration Document	●	●	●	●

ADVANCE PLANNING WEBSITES

www.andalucia.org
www.es.yahoo.com
www.gospain.org
www.vitualtourist.com
www.met-office.gov.uk
www.theaa.com

TOURIST OFFICES AT HOME

In the UK Spanish Tourist Office, 22/23 Manchester Square, London W1M 5AP ☎ (020) 7486 8077; www.tourspain.co.uk

In the USA Tourist Office of Spain, 666 Fifth Avenue 35th, New York, NY 10103 ☎ (212) 265 8822; www.okspain.org

Tourist Office of Spain, 8383 Wilshire Boulevard, Suite 960, Beverley Hills, Cal 90211 ☎ (323) 658 7188; www.okspain.org

HEALTH ADVICE

Insurance

Nationals of EU countries are entitled to some free medical treatment in Spain with the relevant documentation (form EHIC for Britons) although private medical insurance is still advised and is essential for all other visitors.

Dental Services

Dental treatment normally has to be paid for in full as dentists operate privately. A list of dentists can be found in the yellow pages of the telephone directory. Dental treatment should be covered by private medical insurance.

TIME DIFFERENCES

Spain is one hour ahead of Greenwich Mean Time (GMT+1), but from late March until the Saturday before the last Sunday in October, summer time (GMT+2) operates.

WHAT'S ON WHEN

January *Los Reyes Magos* (6 January). In Málaga and all major coastal resorts the Three Kings throw sweets from grand floats.

February/March *Carnaval* (the week before Lent) in Málaga, Granada and Antequera. Floats, colourful costumes, music and dancing.

March/April *Semana Santa* (Holy Week, moveable date) in Sevilla, Málaga and Granada. From Palm Sunday to Easter Sunday there are nightly processions of *cofradías* (brotherhoods) carrying images of the saints or the Virgin; wearing pointed hoods, each carries a lighted candle. The muffled drums are accompanied by the occasional *saeta* (improvised religious lament).

April *Fería de Sevilla* (Seville Fair). Originally a cattle fair, the *fería* has evolved into a world-famous event of colour, music and *flamenco.* The daily horseback parade is a special attraction with the men in dashing outfits and their ladies decked out in traditional flamboyant dresses. Every afternoon bullfights take place in the Maestranza ring with the most famous of Spain's matadors.

May *Las Cruces de Mayo* (early May). This represents an ancient custom when crosses decorated with both real and paper flowers are placed in the streets and squares. The fiesta is particularly attractive in Torrox and Coín.

May/June *Corpus Christi* (moveable date). Processions pass along flower-strewn streets. They are especially colourful in Granada, with parades, music and dancing.

NATIONAL HOLIDAYS

JAN	FEB	MAR	APR	MAY	JUN	JUL	AUG	SEP	OCT	NOV	DEC
2	1	(3)	(3)	1	1	1	1		1	1	3

1 Jan	New Year's Day
6 Jan	Epiphany
28 Feb	Andalusian Day (regional)
Mar/Apr	Maundy Thursday, Good Friday, Easter Monday
1 May	Labour Day
24 Jun	San Juan (regional)
25 Jul	Santiago (regional)
15 Aug	Assumption of the Virgin
12 Oct	National Day
1 Nov	All Saints' Day
6 Dec	Constitution Day
8 Dec	Feast of the Immaculate Conception
25 Dec	Christmas Day

Most shops, offices and museums close on these days.

July *La Virgen del Carmen* (16 July). The most spectacular events are at Los Boliches, Fuengirola; also at Estepona, Marbella and Nerja. The patron saint of fishermen is paraded through the streets before being taken around the bay on a boat; fireworks, music and dancing on the beach.

September *Pedro Romero Fiestas* (early September). Ronda celebrates the bullfighter with *corridas Goyescas* (Goya-style bullfights), with top matadors in costume from Goya's time.

October *Feria del Rosario.* This fair is celebrated in Fuengirola during the first two weeks in October. *Casetas* (clubhouses) of various societies and brotherhoods set up between Fuengirola and Los Boliches offer shows, food and drink. A lively affair, with horseback-riding events, flamenco and fireworks.

December *Fiesta de Verdiales* (29 December). In La Venta de San Cayetano, in Puerto de la Torre, Málaga. Colourfully attired *pandas* (musical groups) compete with each other; a lively event with music, food and wine.

Getting There

BY AIR

Most visitors to the Costa del Sol arrive at Málaga Airport (☎ 952 04 88 38), which is 10km (6 miles) outside the city centre. Spain's national airline, Iberia (☎ 902 40 05 00), operates direct scheduled flights to Málaga from major European and North American cities. The number 19 bus runs into Málaga every 30 minutes (daily 7am to 11.30pm) and takes around 30 minutes. A taxi should cost about €9.

The other nearest airport is Seville (Seville), 8km (5 miles) from the city centre (☎ 954 44 90 00), which handles internal and international flights from London, Amsterdam, Brussels and Paris. A bus into the city runs every 30 minutes (daily 6.45am to 11pm) and takes about 30 minutes. A taxi will cost you around €15.

BY RAIL

Málaga's main station (☎ 902 24 02 02; www.renfe.es) is just 1km (0.6 miles) from the city. However, rail journeys are very time-consuming from other parts of Europe. For example, the journey time from London is around 30 hours and you will need to change in Paris and then again at the Spanish border. You may even need to change again in Madrid. However, once in Madrid, there are a number of possible connections to Seville or Córdoba.

Getting Around

PUBLIC TRANSPORT

INTERNAL FLIGHTS

The national airline, Iberia, plus the smaller Spanair, operate an extensive network of internal flights. Check the websites www.iberia.com and www.spanair.com. Alternatively, both airlines have offices at the airport. National flights are expensive, but worth considering if you are in a hurry.

TRAINS

Services are provided by the state-run company – RENFE. Fares are among the least expensive in Europe. A useful service is the coastal route from Málaga to Fuengirola, via Torremolinos and Benalmádena, with a stop at the airport. Trains run every 30 minutes between 7am and 11pm (RENFE ☎ 902 24 02 02; www.renfe.es).

BUSES

There is a comprehensive and reliable bus network operated by

different companies along the coast and to inland towns and villages. Fares are very reasonable. Go to the local bus station for details of routes. The bus station in Málaga (☎ 952 35 00 61) is just behind the RENFE train station.

FERRIES

A service runs from Málaga to Melilla (in Morocco), run by Trasmediterránea Málaga (☎ 902 45 46 45; www.trasmediterranea.es), taking 10 hours. A shorter route to Morocco is from Algeciras to Ceuta (1.5 hours) and Tangier – via Gibraltar – (2.5 hours) run by Trasmediterránea (☎ 956 66 52 00), and Transtour (☎ 956 65 37 06).

URBAN TRANSPORT

Traffic in the main towns and resorts of the Costa del Sol is normally heavy, especially in summer, but public transport in the form of buses is generally good. From the RENFE station there is a bus which runs every 10 minutes or so to the city centre.

TAXIS

Only use taxis that display a licence issued by the local authority. Taxis show a green light when available for rent. They can be flagged down in the street. In cities and large towns taxis are metered; where they are not, determine the price of the journey in advance.

DRIVING

Driving is on the right. Speed limits on *autopistas* (toll motorways) and *autovías* (free motorways): **120kph** (75mph); dual carriageways and roads with overtaking lanes: **100kph** (62mph). Take care on the N340 coastal highway. Cars travel at tremendous speed and this road is labelled as a dangerous one. Speed limits on country roads: **90kph** (56mph). Speed limits on urban roads: **50kph** (30mph); in residential areas: **20kph** (12.5mph).

Seatbelts must be worn in front seats at all times and in rear seats where fitted.

There is random breath-testing – never drive under the influence of alcohol.

Fuel (*gasolina*) is available in *Sin plomo* (unleaded, 95 and 98 octane); *gasoleo* or *gasoil* (diesel)

and *Super* (96 octane), although this is being phased out so it is not available at all fuel stations. Fuel prices are fixed by the Government and are similar to those in the UK. Most stations take credit cards.

If you break down with your own car and are a member of a motoring organization with a reciprocal agreement (such as the AA in the UK) you can contact the Real Automóvil Club de España, or RACE (☎ 902 40 45 45; www.race.es); which has English-speaking staff and offers 24-hour breakdown assistance. Most international car rental companies provide a rescue service.

CAR RENTAL

The leading international car rental companies operate on the Costa del Sol and you can rent a car in advance (essential at peak periods) either direct or through a travel agent. Airlines may offer 'fly-drive' deals. Renting from a local firm, though, is usually cheaper.

CONCESSIONS

Students/Youths Holders of an International Student Identity Card (ISIC) or Euro 26 card may be able to obtain some concessions on travel, entrance fees etc, but the Costa del Sol is not really geared up for students (special facilities and programmes are limited). The main advantage for students and young people is that low-cost package deals are available.

Senior Citizens The Costa del Sol is an excellent destination for older travellers – travel agents offer tailored package holidays. In the winter months there are special low-cost, long-stay holidays for senior citizens; the best deals are available through tour operators who specialize in holidays for senior citizens.

Being There

TOURIST OFFICES

HEAD OFFICE

- Costa del Sol Tourist Board ☎ 952 05 86 94/95; **www.**visitcostadelsol.com

TOWNS /RESORTS

- Plaza San Sebastian 7, Antequera ☎ 952 70 25 05; **www.**turismoantequera.com
- Avenida Antonio Machado 10, Benalmádena Costa ☎ 952 44 12 95; **www.**benalmadena.com
- Avenida San Lorenzo 1, Estepona ☎ 952 80 09 13; **www.**infoestepona.com
- Avenida Jesús Santos Rein 6, Fuengirola ☎ 952 46 74 57; **www.**fuengirola.org
- Pasaje de Chinitas 4, Málaga ☎ 952 21 34 45; **www.**ayto.malaga.es
- Glorieta de la Fontanilla, Marbella ☎ 952 77 14 42; **www.**marbella.es
- Calle Puerta del Mar 4, Nerja ☎ 952 52 15 31; **www.**nerja.org
- Avenida Marqués del Duero 69, San Pedro de Alcántara ☎ 952 78 52 52
- Avenida de Andalucía 52, Torre del Mar ☎ 952 54 11 04
- Ayuntamiento, Plaza Picasso, Torremolinos ☎ 952 37 95 12; **www.**ayto-torremolinos.org

EMBASSIES AND CONSULATES

UK ☎ 952 35 23 00 (Málaga)
Germany ☎ 952 36 35 91 (Málaga)
USA ☎ 952 47 48 91 (Fuengirola)
Ireland ☎ 952 47 51 08 (Fuengirola)

TELEPHONES

All telephone numbers throughout Spain now consist of nine digits. Most public telephones take coins and phonecards (*tarjetas telefónicas*), which are sold at *tabacos* or post offices for €6 or €12. Some also accept credit cards.

OPENING HOURS

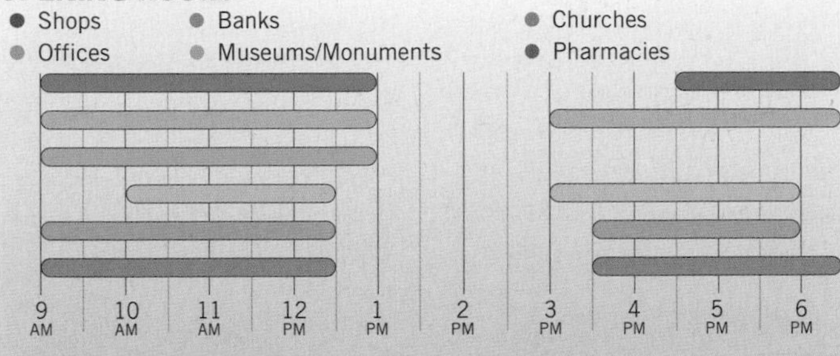

In addition to the times above, department stores, larger supermarkets and shops in tourist resorts open from 10am through to 8, 9 or even 10pm. Most shops close Sunday and some in August. Most banks open 9–2 (Mon–Fri). Some banks also open Sat 9–2 (Oct–May). The opening times of museums can vary: some open longer in summer, while hours may be reduced in winter. Many museums close Sunday afternoon, some also on Saturday afternoon, as well as Monday or another day in the week. Some museums offer free entry to EU citizens (take your passport).

EMERGENCY TELEPHONE NUMBERS

Police (Policía Nacional) 112; (Policía Local) 092
Ambulance (Ambulancia) 061
Fire (Bomberos) 080 or 952 12 66 00 (Málaga); 952 77 43 49 (Marbella); 952 38 39 39 (Torremolinos)

INTERNATIONAL DIALLING CODES

Dial 00 followed by:
UK 44
Germany 49
USA/Canada 1
Netherlands 31

POSTAL SERVICES

Post offices (*correos*) are generally open as below; in main centres they may open extended hours. Málaga's main post office is at Avenida de Andalucía 1. Stamps (*sellos*) can also be bought at tobacconists (*estancos*).
Open: Mon–Sat 9–2 (1pm Sat)
☎ 902 29 72 97 (Málaga)

ELECTRICITY

The power supply is: 220/230 volts (in some bathrooms and older buildings: 110/120 volts).

Round, two-hole sockets take round plugs with two round pins. British visitors will need an adaptor and US visitors a transformer.

CURRENCY

The euro is the single currency of the European Monetary Union, which has been adopted by 12 member states, including Spain. There are banknotes for 5, 10, 20, 50, 100, 200 and 500 euros, and coins for 1, 2, 5, 10, 20 and 50 cents, and 1 and 2 euros. Euro traveller's cheques may be exchanged in banks and exchange offices but the commission may be high and they are not generally acccepted for purchases. Credit cards are widely acccepted and ATMs may be used for cash withdrawal.

HEALTH AND SAFETY

Sun Advice The sunniest (and hottest) months are July and August. Try to avoid the midday sun and use a high-factor sun block at first, and allow yourself to become used to the sun gradually. Protective hats are advisable.

Drugs Prescriptions and non-prescription drugs and medicines are available from pharmacies (*farmácias*), distinguished by a large green cross. They are able to dispense many drugs which would be available only on prescription in other countries.

Safe Water Tap water is chlorinated and generally safe to drink; however, unfamiliar water may cause mild abdominal upsets. Mineral water (*agua mineral*) is cheap and widely available. It is sold *sin gas* (still) and *con gas* (carbonated).

TIPS/GRATUITIES

Yes ✓ No ✕

Restaurants (if service not included)	✓	5%
Cafés/bars	✓	change
Taxis	✓	change
Porters	✓	change
Chambermaids	✓	change
Cloakroom attendants	✓	change
Hairdressers	✓	change
Theatre/cinema usherettes	✓	change
Toilets	✓	change

Petty Crime Snatching of handbags and cameras, pick-pocketing, theft of unattended baggage and car break-ins are the principal crimes against visitors. Any crime or loss should be reported to the national police force (Policía Nacional), who wear brown uniforms. Take the same precautions as you would at home.

PHOTOGRAPHY

Best times to photograph: the summer sun can be too bright so it is best to take photographs in the early morning or late evening.

TRAVELLERS WITH DISABILITIES

Facilities for visitors with disabilities are sparse but there is some progress. Some hotels offer fixed and mobile ramps, lifts, and wider doorways, corridors and toilets to admit wheelchairs. If such services are required, check that the hotel in question carries the wheelchair symbol and state your needs before booking. For further information contact: Mobility Abroad, Benalmádena (☎ 952 44 77 64; www.mobilityabroad.com) – they also rent Mobility Scooters. Lux Mundi, Fuengirola (☎ 952 47 48 40; Independent Living Spain, Mijas Costa (☎ 952 49 34 19; www.independentlivingspain.com).

CLOTHING SIZES

France	UK	Spain & Rest of Europe	USA	
46	36	46	36	Suits
48	38	48	38	
50	40	50	40	
52	42	52	42	
54	44	54	44	
56	46	56	46	
41	7	41	8	Shoes
42	7.5	42	8.5	
43	8.5	43	9.5	
44	9.5	44	10.5	
45	10.5	45	11.5	
46	11	46	12	
37	14.5	37	14.5	Shirts
38	15	38	15	
39/40	15.5	39/40	15.5	
41	16	41	16	
42	16.5	42	16.5	
43	17	43	17	
36	8	34	6	Dresses
38	10	36	8	
40	12	38	10	
42	14	40	12	
44	16	42	14	
46	18	44	16	
38	4.5	38	6	Shoes
38	5	38	6.5	
39	5.5	39	7	
39	6	39	7.5	
40	6.5	40	8	
41	7	41	8.5	

Best
places
to see

1 La Alcazaba, Málaga

The old Moorish fortress, or Alcazaba, dating back to the second half of the 11th century, stands high above the city of Málaga.

Just up from the Plaza de Aduana are the solid, fortified walls of La Alcazaba, landmark of Málaga. The fortress dates back to the 700s, but most of the structure belongs to the mid-11th century. Entrance is through the gateway known as the Puerta del Cristo (Christ's Door), where the first Mass was celebrated following the Christian victory over the town.

The way winds up through attractive gardens, fountains and courtyards, passing through the gateways of Puerta de las Columnas, Arco del Cristo and Arcos de Granada. The terraces have magnificent views of the town and harbour. A small palace within the inner perimeter is the home of the Museo de la Alcazaba, which displays a range of Moorish objects recovered from the area.

Below the entrance to the Alcazaba are the ruins of a Roman amphitheatre dating back to the second century. Much of the old structure can be seen, with restoration nearing completion. Above the Alcazaba stands the castle which crowns the Gibralfaro Hill (► 47).

135 C6 Calle Alcazabilla, s/n 952 22 51 06 Summer Tue–Sun 8.30–8; winter Tue–Sun 8.30–7 Inexpensive Many nearby Centro-Alameda railway station

2 La Alhambra, Granada

One of Spain's greatest splendours, the palace of La Alhambra remains as a legacy of the rich culture brought to the peninsula by the Moors.

The Alhambra holds a commanding position above the city of Granada, backed by the snowcapped peaks of the Sierra Nevada. Built by the Moors between the 13th and 15th centuries, it was used as a residence by Muhammad I, and members of the Nasrid dynasty. In 1984 it joined UNESCO's list of World Heritage Sites.

Walk up to the entrance from the Plaza Nueva. To the east is the Renaissance palace of Emperor Carlos V, started in 1526 but never completed. To the west is the Alcazaba, the oldest building on the site. Climb to the top of the Vela tower for breath-taking views of Granada and the Sierra Nevada.

A tour of the interior of the Casa Real (Royal Palace) reveals the true marvels: the beautifully decorated Patio de Mexuar, the pretty Patio de los Arrayanes (named after the myrtle trees that line a rectangular pool), and the Salón de los Embajadores (Ambassadors' Hall) with its richly carved and coffered ceiling. The Sala de los Abencerrajes has an impressive stalactite ceiling, and the Sala de las Dos Hermanas (Hall of the Two Sisters) features a delicate honeycomb dome. The focal point is the Patio de los Leones (Courtyard of Lions), named after the figures around the fountain.

On the nearby Cerro del Sol (Hill of the Sun) stands the Palacio del Generalife. Dating back to the early 1300s, it was the summer palace of the Moorish kings. The gardens exude an aura of romance, with pools and fountains amid greenery, flowers and the resident cats.

123 C7 Calle Real, s/n, Granada 958 02 7900 Mar–Oct daily 8.30–8. Night visits Tue–Sat 8.30–6, Fri, Sat 8–9.30. Access to the Palacios Nazaries 8–8.45 Moderate; free Sun after 3pm for visitors with disabilities, senior citizens Few Alhambrabus from town centre Booking tickets is strongly recommended either via www.alhambratickets.com or through branches of Banco Bilbao Vizcaya Argentaria (BBV). A limited number of tickets are sold daily on site but sell out quickly

3 Casares

With its mass of whitewashed houses sprawling up the hillside, Casares has acquired a reputation for being the most photogenic town in Andalucía.

From whichever angle you approach, the views of Casares are spectacular. The town is easily accessible from the coast: a turning around 16km (10 miles) west of Estepona leads up into the hills of the Sierra Bermeja. While the drive itself takes you through a scenic route of hills and wooded areas, nothing prepares you for the spectacular

view of Casares with its white houses spread over the hill crowned by a Moorish castle. The town saw many battles between the warring Muslims, until it was taken by the Christians in the mid-15th century.

Much of the charm of Casares can be discovered by strolling through its terraced streets to the castle above. On the way up, take a look at the 17th-century Church of San Sebastian, which contains a statue of the Virgen del Rosario del Campo. The castle was built in the 13th century on Roman foundations. The nearby 16th-century Church of the Incarnation retains its original Mudéjar tower.

The views become more spectacular as you continue to the summit, where you will be rewarded by a panorama over olive groves, orchards and forests to the blue of the Mediterranean Sea. Take a look at the local cemetery, which is beautifully kept and adorned with flowers.

121 D5 105km (65 miles) west of Málaga Several restaurants Local buses August Fair (early Aug)
Calle Villa 29, Casares 952 89 41 26

4 Casco Antiguo, Marbella

The jewel of Marbella is its Casco Antiguo (Old Town), a picturesque maze of narrow streets, whitewashed houses and pretty squares.

To the north of Avenida Ramón y Cajal, which cuts through the town, Marbella's old quarter is a delightful area in which to browse with its flower-filled streets, neat little houses and small squares. Among its prettiest streets are Remedios, Dolores, Rincón de la Virgen and San Cristóbal, noted for the brilliance of their flower displays.

Sooner or later everyone converges on the Plaza de los Naranjos, a lovely square lined with orange trees. This is a popular place for a drink or alfresco meal where you can enjoy people-watching and the streetlife. In the middle of the square is a bust of a serene King Juan Carlos.

Evidence of the town's Moorish, Christian and Roman past can be seen on many of its buildings. Take a look at the Iglesia de la Incarnación and, above it, the remaining towers of an old Moorish fortress; the 16th-century Ayuntamiento (Town Hall), home of the tourist office, the Casa Consistorial, which has a fine Mudéjar entrance and the Ermita de Nuestro Señor Santiago, Marbella's earliest Christian church. Worth a glimpse, too, is the attractive little Cofradía del Santo Christo de Amor chapel, at one end of the Plaza de los Naranjos. A stroll through this area is particularly enjoyable in spring when the heady scent of orange blossom fills the air.

121 D6 Marbella (56km/35 miles west of Málaga) Many restaurants (€–€€€) Marbella bus stop, Avenida Ricardo Soriano 21 (Bus station Avenida del Trapiche, s/n) Pre-Lent Carnival; Fería de San Bernabé (11–18 Jun)

5 Cuevas de Nerja

This series of caverns, close to the coastal town of Nerja, has spectacular rock formations and palaeolithic paintings.

These limestone caves were discovered by chance in 1959 by a group of boys who were out and about exploring. Beyond the first grotto, great caverns revealed a wonderful world of stalactites and stalagmites, and various items such as stone tools and fragments of pottery. Investigations show that the area must have been inhabited by man more than 20,000 years ago. A group of sculptures near the entrance to the caves honours the boys who made the discovery.

The rock paintings of horses, deer, goats and dolphins are not open for public viewing, but photographs of them are on display, together with

objects found here. However, the main attraction is the display of formations enhanced by special lighting effects.

The first chamber provides a magnificent setting for concerts, which are held here as part of an annual summer festival. The next cavern is called the Hall of Ghosts after a strange shroud-like figure that appears in the stone. Most impressive of the caves is the huge Hall of Cataclysms, which features the tallest column of its kind in the world, rising from a mass of stalactites.

123 D6 4km (2.5 miles) east of Nerja 952 52 95 20 Summer daily 10–2, 4–8; winter daily 10–2, 4–6.30 Inexpensive Restaurant (€€) Best by car Summer concerts and ballet performances

6 La Giralda y La Catedral, Sevilla

The minaret tower known as La Giralda, seen as a symbol of Sevilla, rises proudly above the great cathedral, the third largest in Europe.

The 98m-high (320ft) brick tower of La Giralda is a prominent feature of Sevilla. It was built in the 12th century as the minaret of the former Great Mosque. In 1565 a section with 25 bells was added and topped with a bronze statue representing Faith, which acts as a *giralda* (weather vane). Climb up to the belfry for magnificent views over the city. Note that there are ramps, not stairs, so it is relatively easy on the knees.

The grand cathedral was built in the Gothic style, with some Renaissance influences. The interior is awe-inspiring for its sheer size and the richness of its decoration, with Gothic columns supporting massive arches that reach up to the great heights of the vaulted ceiling.

A handsome 16th-century grille in the Sanctuary encloses an immense golden Gothic altarpiece which rates as one of the cathedral's greatest glories and is said to be the largest altar in the world. Started by the Flemish artist Dancart in 1482, it took almost a hundred years to complete the 45 tableaux depicting the lives of Jesus and Mary.

The choirstalls are fine examples of Flamboyant Gothic. Notable also is the Capilla Real (Royal Chapel); completed in 1575, it features a richly decorated Renaissance cupola. On either side are the tombs of King Alfonso X (the Wise) and his mother, Beatrice of Swabia. In the south transept is the ornate tomb of Christopher Columbus, whose body lay here after it was transported from Cuba.

116 C4 Plaza Virgen de los Reyes 954 21 49 71 Jul–Aug Mon–Sat 9.30–3.30, Sun 2.30–6; Sep–Jun Mon–Sat 11–5, Sun 2–6 Moderate; Sun free Many restaurants nearby RENFE station
Sevilla (➤ 85)

7 La Mezquita, Córdoba

The great mosque of Córdoba stands as a remarkable achievement and monument to Moorish architecture.

The Mezquita of Córdoba was built in four stages between the 8th and 10th centuries and is among the world's largest mosques, remaining as a testimony to the immense power of Islam at the height of its domination of the peninsula.

Do not be discouraged by the mosque's somewhat forbidding outward appearance: its beauty lies within. The main entrance is through the Puerta del Perdón, which leads into the Patio de los Naranjos (Courtyard of the Oranges). Once inside you are confronted by a forest of columns of onyx, marble and granite. The light effects within this dim interior are sensational. The columns are topped by decorated capitals and crowned by the striking red and white arches so characteristic of Moorish architecture. There is a sense of awe and mysticism, special to this particular mosque, which lures the visitor back time and time again.

To find a Christian cathedral within the very heart of the mosque comes as a surprise. It was built in the 1520s on the orders of Hapsburg Emperor Carlos V, who later regretted his decision. However, it does blend fairly well into its surroundings.

Rising above the Puerta del Perdón is the bell tower, which offers splendid views of the city.

118 B4 Torrijos y Cardenal Herrero 957 47 05 12 Mon–Sat 10–6.30, Sun 2–6.30 Moderate Many restaurants nearby (€–€€€) RENFE station, Avenida de America, Córdoba

Córdoba (➤ 67)

8 Mijas

With its attractive mountain setting, narrow streets and whitewashed houses, Mijas is a popular excursion from the coast.

Despite the fact that Mijas caters so obviously for the tourist it has retained its charm. The little town is undeniably pretty, with its white houses, narrow winding streets, flowers and plants. The setting is lovely, with magnificent views of the surrounding pine-clad mountains and the coast. Its proximity to the coast, a drive of some 20 minutes or so, makes it an ideal destination for a day's excursion.

On the central square of the Plaza de la Virgen you will see the ever-patient donkeys lined up. Adorned with colourful saddles and tassles, they can be hired for rides around town, serving as donkey taxis. Concerts and fiestas are sometimes held in the square, which centres around a small fountain and is a popular meeting place. Opposite, a large underground parking area has greatly helped to ease traffic problems.

Near the square is a neat little park with fine views. Hollowed out from a chunk of rock is a small chapel known as the Santuario de la Virgen de la Peña Limosnas. Inside is the image of Santa Maria de la Peña, along with some impressive candlesticks, embroidered garments and other religious relics.

A stroll to the Plaza de la Constitución leads past the Miniature Museum 'Carromato de Max', which has a collection of tiny curios. Up the slope from the plaza stands the charming little Parish Church of La Inmaculada Concepción, built mostly in the Mozarabic style. Nearby is the town's small, rectangular bullring.

121 D7 37km (23 miles) west of Málaga Many restaurants (€–€€€) Local bus services St Anthony's Day (16–17 Jan); Feria de la Virgen de la Peña (early Sep); Romería de Santa Teresa (end Oct)
Ayuntamiento, Plaza Virgen de la Peña, s/n
952 48 59 00

9 Puente Nuevo, Ronda

The old town of Ronda is famed for its spectacular setting and views from the bridge over the El Tajo ravine.

Ronda is one of Spain's oldest cities. Situated within the rugged landscape of the Serranía de Ronda, the town is split in two, divided by the gorge of the River Guadalevín, which is spanned by the Puente Nuevo (New Bridge). The city has long held a deep fascination with writers and painters and the scene of Ronda perched on the clifftop with the bridge spanning the gorge has been the subject of countless paintings and photographs. Today, the dramatic views from the bridge, combined with the attractions of the old town and its historical interest, continue to make Ronda (➤ 78–79) a top excursion for visitors staying along the coast.

The Puente Nuevo (which has become the city's symbol) was begun in 1751 and completed in 1793. It stands a full 96m (315ft) above the Tajo gorge at its highest and narrowest point. Sadly, the bridge's architect did not live to see its completion, tragically dying after falling out of a basket while inspecting its construction.

121 C6 118km (73 miles) northwest of Málaga
Many restaurants in Ronda (€–€€€) Buses from Algeciras, Cádiz, Málaga (via Torremolinos, Marbella, San Pedro) and Sevilla
Ronda (➤ 79)

10 Puerto Banús

The dazzling marina of Puerto Banús, with its luxurious yachts and sophisticated restaurants and bars, serves as a magnet for visitors to the Costa del Sol.

A stay on the Costa del Sol would be incomplete without a visit to Puerto Banús, one of the Costa's most famous attractions. Built in 1968, this luxurious port, the creation of promoter José Banús, was one of Spain's first village-type harbour developments.

Backed by the mountains, a ring of brilliant white apartment houses surrounds the marina, which is filled with craft of all sizes, from mega yachts to

small sailing boats. A feature of Banús is the complex of luxury apartments, located on the right as you enter the port. With its opulent marble façade and gleaming turrets, the inspiration could have been taken straight from the *Arabian Nights*.

Around the port is a string of cafés, bars and restaurants, along with boutiques and gift shops. While frontline restaurants are *the* places in which to be seen, better value is sometimes found in some of the small restaurants in the streets behind, tucked away up flights of stairs. In season the quayside is thronged with people who come to see, or to be seen – this can be a great place for celebrity-spotting. The Saladuba Pub and the Sinatra Bar are favourite haunts for hanging out.

At night the place becomes a hive of activity, as the smart restaurants, slick piano bars and clubs fill up with the chichi set. While the glamour of its earlier days may have dimmed, Banús still rates as a star attraction.

121 D6 64km (40 miles) west of Málaga, 6km (4 miles) west of Marbella Many bars and restaurants (€€–€€€) Bus services from Marbella and San Pedro de Alcántara

Avenida Principal, s/n 952 11 38 30 (summer only)

Exploring

The Costa del Sol falls into two parts with Málaga forming the divide between the western and eastern sections. The most developed and best-known area is west of Málaga, starting with Torremolinos and including the major resorts of Benalmádena Costa, Fuengirola, Marbella and Estepona. This part of the coastline is virtually one long stream of apartment blocks, marina developments, hotels and restaurants. The eastern Costa del Sol, stretching towards Almería, has a totally different appeal. Here the coastline is often broken up by rocks and small coves and is much less developed, with Nerja standing out as a favoured resort. The interior offers excursions to white Andalucían villages nestling in the mountains, and to the great cities of Granada, Córdoba and Sevilla.

Málaga

Málaga is the second city of Andalucía and capital of the Costa del Sol, forming a natural divide between its western and eastern sections. The town is crowned by the old Moorish castle that stands atop the Gibralfaro Hill, holding a commanding view of Málaga's harbour and the wide sweep of the bay.

The backing of the Montes de Málaga mountain range provides shelter from the wind, ensuring a pleasant Mediterranean climate, which is particularly agreeable from autumn through to spring. To many tourists Málaga has tended to serve primarily as a gateway to the coast or its hinterland. Now, with the opening of the Picasso Museum, along with several other new museums and expansion projects, there is an awakening of interest in the city whose old quarters, churches, traditional bars and restaurants give a true taste of Andalucía.

LA ALCAZABA

See pages 22–23.

CASA NATAL DE PICASSO

Spain's celebrated painter Pablo Ruiz Picasso was born in 1881 in the corner house of an elegant yellow-toned block on the Plaza de la Merced. His birthplace was declared an historic-artistic monument in 1983, and in 1991 it became the headquarters of the Pablo Ruiz Picasso Foundation. The centre was created to foster cultural activities, including the promotion of contemporary art with a special emphasis on Picasso himself.

The exhibition, covering two floors, includes early sketches by the artist, plus sculptures, photos and family memorabilia.

It was here that Picasso began to paint, helped by his father, an art teacher, who had recognized his young son's talent.
122 D4 Plaza de la Merced 15 952 06 02 15 Mon–Sat 11–2, 5–8, Sun 10–2 Inexpensive Many nearby (€–€€€) Centro-Alameda railway station

CASTILLO DE GIBRALFARO

Right above the Alcazaba stands the Castillo de Gibralfaro, crowning the hill of the same name. It was built by Yusef I of Granada at the beginning of the 14th century on a former Phoenician site and lighthouse from which its name was derived – *gebel-faro* (rock of the lighthouse) signifies the beacon that served to guide ships into the harbour.

This was once the scene of a three-month siege by the citizens of Málaga against the Catholic Monarchs Ferdinand and Isabella. The matter was concluded only when hunger led to capitulation, after which Ferdinand occupied the site while his queen took up residence in the town. All that remains today of this historic monument is a series of solid ramparts which rise majestically among dense woods of pines and eucalyptus, with the Alcazaba not far below.

Although it can be reached on foot from the Alcazaba, it's better to get to the castle by bus, car or even horse and carriage. You can round off a visit with a cool drink at the Parador de Málaga, which also offers panoramic views of the harbour and city, with landmarks such as the cathedral and bullring.
125 C7 Gibralfaro Mountain 952 22 00 43 Daily 9–6 Inexpensive *Parador* nearby 35

a walk through the Old Town

This walk starts in the Plaza de la Marina and makes a tour of Málaga's old areas, taking in the cathedral and several churches.

From the Plaza de la Marina take Calle Molina Lario, left of the Málaga Palacio Hotel which faces you. A few moments' walk will bring you right up to the cathedral.

Horses and carriages line up here ready to take visitors on a tour around the town. Opposite, on the Plaza Obispo, is the old Palacio Episcopal, which contains some delightful 'hidden' patios and has exhibitions of contemporary art.

Turn right along Calle Santa Maria to take Calle San Agustín.

On your right is the Palacio Buenavista, which now houses the Museo Picasso (➤ 55).

Take a right fork into Calle Granada which takes you by the Iglesia de Santiago. Almost opposite is tiny Tomás de

Cózar 13 leading to Málaga's El Hammam Arab baths. Continue along Calle Granada to the Plaza de la Merced.

The centre of the plaza is marked by an obelisk in memory of General Torrijos and his men who were shot after the War of Independence. On the far corner, in a block of houses, is the Casa Natal de Picasso (► 46–47), birthplace of Pablo Picasso, now centre of the Picasso Foundation.

Return down Calle Granada to the Plaza del Siglo and on to the Plaza de la Constitucíon, then stroll down Calle Marqués Larios, Málaga's main shopping street. Down on the left make a short detour through the archway and along Pasaje de Chinitas, which leads to a square. Complete the walk down Calle Larios and turn into the Alameda Principal to the Plaza de la Marina.

Distance 4km (2.5 miles)
Time 3–4 hours, depending on stops
Start/end point Plaza de la Marina 124 C4
Lunch La Posada de Antonio (€€) Esparteros 4
952 17 26 29

CATEDRAL

Málaga's cathedral is large and has a somewhat sombre exterior. It was built between 1528 and 1782 on or near the site of a former mosque. While original plans had allowed for two towers, lack of funds resulted in the completion of only one, giving rise to the name by which the cathedral is affectionately referred to, La Manquita, loosely interpreted as 'the little one-armed woman'. The interior has influences of the Renaissance and baroque styles. The notable 17th-century choir stalls of mahogany and cedarwood were designed by Luis Ortíz. After his death the 40 finely carved statues of the saints behind each stall were completed by Pedro de Mena, one of Spain's most celebrated wood-carvers of the time, who spent some years in Málaga. Some of the chapels leading off the aisles also contain works by Pedro de Mena and his tutor Alonso Cano.

Adjoining the cathedral is the Iglesia del Sagrario. Founded in the 15th century on the site of a mosque, the church has an unusual rectangular shape. Its Isabelline-Gothic portal is the only remaining part of the original structure, which was rebuilt in 1714. The interior is richly decorated and its main altar features a magnificent 16th-century retable.

125 C5 Calle Molina Larios, s/n 952 21 59 17 Mon–Sat 10–6.45 Inexpensive None Centro-Alameda railway station

CENTRO (CENTRE)

The heart of Málaga lies north of the Alameda Principal, Málaga's main avenue, and east of the Río Guadalmedina, which separates the old town from the new. As soon as you turn off the Alameda you enter a labyrinthine medieval world of narrow, twisting roads. There is much to be enjoyed here, increasingly so the more you find your bearings. The centre is small and many streets are pedestrian-only, so exploring on foot is both enjoyable and viable.

Another way in which to enjoy a tour around town is by horse-drawn carriage, a good option if you are tired or feeling the heat. You will see these lined up by the cathedral, in the Paseo del Parque and various other points around the town.

While the cathedral is a focal point from which to start exploring, the main artery of the city centre is the elegant shopping street Calle Marqués de Larios, which leads from the Alameda Principal north to the Plaza de la Constitución. On either side are narrow streets and small squares where you can happily browse for hours. Within this area are a number of churches and a few museums, all within close range. You will also discover picturesque narrow streets lined with bars, cafés and shops.

Málaga is famed for its *tapas* bars. For some local atmosphere try one on the so-called *rutas del tapeo* (*tapas* route) which covers the area west of Calle Marqués de Larios, centering around Calle Nueva.

124 B4 Huge choice of restaurants (€–€€€)

CENTRO DE ARTE CONTEMPORÁNEO DE MÁLAGA

CAC Málaga includes contemplative photographic studies and paintings, some of them immense and all given optimum display space in this former warehouse. The aim is to pioneer ultramodern artistic trends through four exhibitions: two temporary; another dedicated to up-and-coming Spanish artists; and a changeable, permanent exhibition.

www.cacmalaga.org

124 D7 Calle Alemania, s/n 952 12 00 55 Summer Tue–Sun 10–2, 5–9; winter Tue–Sun 10–8 Free Centro-Alameda railway station

IGLESIA DE LOS MÁRTIRES

The church was founded in 1487 and dedicated to the martyrs of the town. It features a striking Mudéjar tower which was added later and a richly decorated baroque-style interior, which includes a sculpture by Francisco Ortíz of Jesus praying on the Mount of Olives.

124 A4 Plaza Mártires 952 21 27 24 Daily 10–2.30, 6–7.30 Free

IGLESIA DE SANTIAGO

Founded in 1490, the church is noted for its tall, Mudéjar-style steeple and baroque interior which contains some notable chapels. Pablo Picasso's baptismal certificate is stored here.

125 B5 Calle Granada 62 952 21 03 99 Daily 9–1.30, 6–9 Free

IGLESIA DEL SANTO CRISTO DE LA SALUD

The interior of this 17th-century church is a real gem. Note the brilliant altarpiece and beautifully decorated cupola. The church also contains the tomb of architect Pedro de la Mena.

124 B4 Calle Compania 952 21 34 56 Free

IGLESIA SAN JUAN BAUTISTA

Founded in 1490, the church's baroque-style tower above the main entrance was added in 1770. Inside are several fine chapels and a rich altarpiece. The 17th-century figure of San Juan is the work of Francisco Ortíz.

124 B3 Calle San Juan, 3 952 21 12 83 Daily 8.30–1, 6–8 Free

JARDÍN BOTÁNICO 'LA CONCEPCIÓN'

Just outside Málaga, Finca de la Concepción is a magnificent botanical garden. You can follow a marked path through exotic trees and plants, passing Roman sculpture and a waterfall.

125 A5 (off map) Along the N331 to Antequera, just off the Málaga ring road 952 25 21 48 Summer Tue–Sun 10–6.30; winter Tue–Sun 10–4 Inexpensive

MUSEO DE ARTES Y COSTUMBRES POPULARES

This little museum is housed in the Mesón de la Victoria, a former 17th-century inn, now attractively restored. The museum is on two floors and was created to give an insight into the past ways and customs of the people of the region.

The first rooms, which display agricultural items, open out onto a courtyard with tropical plants. In the rooms beyond you can see a fishing boat and some interiors of old houses. Upstairs, displays include collections of costumes, ceramics and tiles, old posters announcing fiestas, religious items and a little group of clay figures depicting a *panda de verdiales* (group of regional musicians).

124 B3 Pasillo de Santa Isabel 10 952 21 71 37 Summer Mon–Fri 10–1, 5–8, Sat 10–12; rest of year Mon–Fri 10–1, 4–7 Inexpensive Railway station Centro-Alameda

MUSEO PICASSO

The Picasso Museum is installed in the Palacio Buenavista, former home of the Palace of Fine Arts. It contains more than 180 works by the artist, including drawings, engravings, lithographs, sculptures and ceramics, the majority of which have been donated by Christina, Picasso's daughter-in-law. There are also temporary exhibitions and displays.

125 B5 Palacio de Buenavista, Calle San Augustín, 8 902 44 33 77 Tue–Thu 10–8, Fri and Sat 10–9 Moderate

a walk around the churches & museums of Málaga

This leisurely walk includes Málaga's main market, an attractive small museum and several churches.

From the Alameda Principal cross over at the traffic lights at the start of the flower market and turn into Calle Torregarda to the Mercado de Atarazas, Malaga's main market.

Pass through the market to take a look at the displays of fruit and vegetables and, in particular, the wonderful selection of glistening fresh fish.

Emerge into the Plaza de Arriola and continue along the Paseo Santa Isabel.

You will find yourself on the banks of the dried up Río Guadalmedina. Look out for a flight of steps on your right that leads down through a tiny garden to the Museo de Artes Populares (➤ 54).

Continue along the Paseo Santa Isabel and turn right down Calle Cisneros.

This brings you into a picturesque part of the old town where a right turn down a narrow alleyway leads to the Iglesia San Juan (➤ 54), standing on a small square.

Retrace your steps, turn right onto Calle Especerías, left along Calle Salvago, left again and right to the Plaza San Ignacio.

Take a look at the Iglesia del Corazón de Jesús. Turn back and take the Calle de los Mártires. On the small square that follows you cannot miss the striking Mudéjar tower of the Iglesia de los Mártires.

Return and turn left along Calle Compañia, past the Iglesia de Santo Cristo de la Salud.

Wander through the Plaza de la Constitución and take the Calle Nueva into the heart of the famous area for *tapas* bars. Some refreshments will no doubt be welcome here. The Calle Puerta del Mar leads straight down to the Alameda Principal and back to the station.

Distance 3.5km (2 miles)
Time 3–4 hours, depending on visits
Start/end point Alameda Principal 124 C3
Lunch Mesón la Aldea (€) Esparteros, 5 952 22 76 89

PALACIO DE LA ADUANA

The Hall of Columns (Salón de Columnas), in this neoclassical former Customs House, which was on the waterfront until the construction of the Paseo del Parque, now exhibits parts of the art collection from the Museum of Fine Arts (Museo de Bellas Artes). The exhibitions and displays are changed at regular intervals. Eventually the whole collection will be rehoused in a new Palace of Fine Arts.

125 C5 Paseo del Parque 952 21 36 80 Tue 3–3, Wed–Fri 9–8, Sat–Sun 9–3 Free Centro-Alameda railway station

EL PARQUE

Málaga's city park, which runs alongside the Paseo del Parque, was created at the end of the 19th century on land reclaimed from the sea. The park contains tropical flowering trees and shrubs. Many of the unusual and exotic species were brought from overseas when Málaga was an important trading centre.

125 D5 Between Paseo del Parque and Paseo de Espana None Daily Free

SANTUARIO DE LA VICTORIA

The church was erected in 1487 on the site where the Catholic Monarchs pitched their tents during the siege of that year. A major feature is the magnificent retable which rises above the main altar. High up, amid a flourish of exuberant ornamentation, is a small *camerín* (chapel) containing a statue of the Madonna and Child (reached by stairs at the far end of the church). In the crypt is the family vault of the counts of Buenavista, who were responsible for the rebuilding of the church in the 17th century.

125 B8 (off map) Plaza del Santuario 952 25 26 47 Tue–Fri 10–12, 4.30–7, Sat 10–12 Free Centro-Alameda railway station

West of Málaga

This is the most popular part of the Costa del Sol, which attracts mass tourism to the crowded and lively resorts of Torremolinos and Fuengirola. But this long ribbon of holiday development backed by wonderful mountain scenery has lots more to offer.

Fashionable haunts such as Puerto Banús and Marbella have an upmarket image and offer excitement and glamour. Smaller, typically Spanish towns, such as Sotogrande and San Pedro de Alcántara, provide the chance to relax in the shade of a pretty plaza. Or you can seek out solitude in one of the remote clifftop villages and towns scattered across the peaks and valleys inland from the coast. The modern city of Sevilla, the capital of Andalucía, has an abundance of culture and fine architecture as well as great shopping opportunities. The diversity, plus wonderful sandy beaches and almost year-long sunshine, is what makes this stretch of coastline so alluring and why visitors return again and again.

ANTEQUERA

Antequera is known for its convents, churches and elegant mansions. It is easily reached by means of the good motorway from Málaga and can be visited in a day (Town Walk ➤ 62–63 and Drive from Torremolinos ➤ 90–91).

The town is dominated by the old castle, which has excellent views of the surrounding plains. The 16th-century Church of Santa María la Mayor, nearby, features a fine Mudéjar ceiling. Dominant are the bell towers of the churches of San Sebastian and San Augustín, which combine the Mudéjar and baroque styles. Outstanding is the Church of El Carmen, which has been designated a national monument. Formerly a convent, it is noted for its rich interior and impressive wooden altar.

The discovery of prehistoric tombs in nearby caves has given the town added importance. Of the three caves here, the most important is the **Dólmen de Menga.** Its large cavern contains a series of stones and columns which support huge slabs that form the roof, believed to date back to *c*2500 BC.

The Parque Nacional El Torcal de Antequera is some 16km (10 miles) south of Antequera and covers an extended area of grey limestone rocks and boulders, weathered with time to form the most weird and wonderful shapes. There is a small information office by the parking area and a magnificent view from the nearby Mirador el Ventanillo. Walking trails are marked by arrows (yellow for a shorter walk, red for a longer one).

www.antequera.es

121 C8 54km (33.5 miles) north of Málaga Good choice of restaurants (€–€€€) From Málaga From Málaga Fería de Primavera (31 May to 1 or 2 Jun); Noche Flamenca de Santa Maria (end Jul); August Fair (early Aug) Plaza San Sebastian 7 952 70 25 05

Dólmen de Menga

1km (0.6 miles) east of Antequera Wed–Sat 9–6, Tue, Sun 9–3.30 Free From Antequera From Antequera

BENALMÁDENA COSTA

Benalmádena Costa is a natural extension of Torremolinos, taking over where Torremolinos leaves off. It covers a long stretch of coast lined with the type of high-rise apartment blocks that characterize this section of the Costa del Sol, along with a string of restaurants, cafés, bars and shops. An attractive seafront promenade makes it possible to walk from Torremolinos all the way along the coast to Benalmádena's Puerto Deportivo (► 65) – you need time and energy for this!

The area has been noticeably upgraded, partly due to the Casino and the 18-hole Torrequebrada golf course, a short distance up into the hills. There are also facilities for waterskiing, jetskiing, windsurfing, sailing and all the popular water sports.

www.benalmadena.com

121 D8 20km (12 miles) west of Málaga Numerous restaurants and bars (€–€€€) Connections Railway station Benalmádena–Arroyo de la Miel Virgen del Carmen fiesta (16 Jul)

Avenida Antonio Machado 10 952 44 12 95

a walk

a stroll around Antequera's churches and mansions

This walk takes in some of Antequera's many churches and includes magnificent views. Most churches close from 1.30 to 4pm so a morning walk is recommended. On the Plaza San Sebastian look at the 16th-century Colegiata de San Sebastian. Walk up Calle Infante Don Fernando. Take a look at the Iglesia de San Agustín, on the left, and farther along, on the right, you will pass the Palacio Consistorial (Town Hall) and the Convento de los Remedios.

Just past the Iglesia de San Juan de Dios turn sharp right into Calle Cantareros and back towards the centre.

You will pass the house of the Condado de Colchado and the Convento de la Madre de Dios de Monteagudo.

Continue down Calle Diego Ponce, then turn left up to Plaza San Francisco and the Plazuela de San Zoilo.

This brings you to the Convento Real de San Zoilo, one of Antequera's National Monuments, and some fine views.

Take Calle Calzada and continue up Cuesta de Los Rojos to Plaza del Carmen. On Calle del Carmen is the Iglesia del Carmen. Return and take a sharp right, turn up Calle del Colegio, a very steep climb, to the Arco de los Gigantes (Arch of Giants) on your left.

Pass through the arch to the Real Colegiata de Santa Maria la Mayor. Nearby are the Roman Baths.

Return through the arch and go left along Calle Herradores to the charming Plaza del Portichuelo, on which stands the Iglesia de Santa Maria de Jesús.

Distance 4.5km (3 miles)
Time About 3 hours
Start point Plaza San Sebastian
121 C8
End point Plaza del Portichuelo
121 C8
Lunch Restaurante El Angelote (€€) Plaza Coso Viejo
952 70 34 65

BENALMÁDENA PUEBLO

Two small inland communities present a complete contrast to the attractions on the coastal strip of Benalmádena Costa. About 1km (0.6 miles) into the hills is Arroyo de la Miel which has developed into quite a lively centre with modern housing, shops and restaurants. Just up the road is the Tivoli World amusement park.

Farther up the hill is Benalmádena Pueblo, whose origins are thought to date back to Phoenician times. This is a charming village of narrow twisting streets and whitewashed houses. With attractive views of the coast and surrounding landscapes, it offers a rural atmosphere. The Museo Arqueológico contains some pre-Columbian exhibits, along with objects from Roman and early Iberian times.

121 D8 · 3km (2 miles) west of Arroyo de la Miel · Variety of restaurants and bars · Local fair (15 Aug); Fería de San Juan (24 Jun) at Arroyo de la Miel

BENALMÁDENA PUERTO MARINA

Benalmádena's Puerto Marina, or Puerto Deportivo as it is known, has developed into one of the most prominent of the marinas that have sprung up along the coast.

Built initially as a small harbour surrounded by a ring of whitewashed houses, Andalucían-style, it has gradually grown into an impressive marina, with more than 1,000 berths. Numerous shops, open-air bars and restaurants line the quayside. A centrepiece is provided by a complex of luxurious apartments called Las Islas de Puerto Marina. Constructed in flamboyant style, they do appear like islands floating on the water.

The marina makes a good outing for all age groups. An outstanding attraction is Sea Life Benalmádena, which can be enjoyed by the whole family. You can also catch a ferry from here to Fuengirola (10.30, 12.30, 2.30, 4.30) or Málaga (10, 1, 4) and enjoy the coastline from the sea.

With its open-air cafés, restaurants and shops, Puerto Marina continues to increase in popularity, especially at weekends, attracting Spaniards and visitors alike with further expansion planned. An ultra-modern underwater lighting system, installed in the waters of the harbour, creates a magical effect at night.

121 D8 Benalmádena Costa Variety of restaurants, bars and pubs

CASARES

See pages 26–27.

Córdoba

Córdoba is one of Andalucía's richest jewels. In addition to the Mezquita or Great Mosque (➤ 34–35), the city's old quarter of narrow streets with flower-filled balconies and patios allows visitors an insight into the essence of southern Spain. The town lies along the banks of the River Guadalquivir, overlooked by the Sierra de Córdoba. With extremes of heat in the summer and harsh winters, a good time to visit is spring or autumn.

Tools found on the banks of the River Guadalquivir suggest that palaeolithic man lived here. Córdoba later became a leading centre of the people of Tartessos and was then conquered by the Carthaginians, the Romans (when it became the capital of Baetica) and the Moors.

In 929, under Moorish rule, the Caliphate of Córdoba was established. With the founding of a university, Córdoba became a renowned hub of art, culture and learning. This period saw the construction of Córdoba's great Mezquita and other fine examples of Moorish architecture.

Gradually, in the 11th and 12th centuries, Córdoba went into decline. With the breaking up of the Caliphate into small *tarifas* (states), Córdoba came under the jurisdiction of Sevilla. After it fell to the Christians in 1236, the Catholic Monarchs presided here while planning the reconquest of Granada and it was here that Queen Isabella granted Columbus the commission for his voyage of discovery.

The city has many attractions and should be explored on foot. Bear in mind that some of its narrow streets do not easily accommodate pedestrians and cars simultaneously! The Judería (old Jewish Quarter) is a delightful area of narrow cobbled streets and white houses. Brilliantly coloured flowers adorn small squares and beautiful ornate patios can be seen through doorways.

www.turiscordoba.es

118 b4 187km (116 miles) north of Málaga Choice of

restaurants (€–€€€) Estación de Autobuses, Plaza de las Tres Culturas 957 40 40 40 Estación de RENFE, Avenida de América 902 24 02 02 Cordoba Patios competition (May), Easter ceremonies; Fair (May); International Festival of Music, Theatre and Dance (Aug); National Festival of Folklore (Sep)
Calle Torrijos 10 957 47 12 35

WHAT TO SEE IN CÓRDOBA

ALCÁZAR DE LOS REYES CRISTIANOS

This Mudéjar-style palace was begun by King Alfonso XI in the early 14th century. Outstanding Roman mosaics, the old Moorish courtyard and baths still remain. This was once the residence of the Catholic Monarchs, and a one-time Moorish prison.
Campo Santo de los Mártires 957 42 01 51 Tue–Sat 10–2, 4.30–6.30; Sun 9.30–2.30 Inexpensive; free Fri

LA MEZQUITA

See pages 34–35.

MUSEO ARQUEOLÓGICO

Housed in the attractive 16th-century Palacio de los Páez, the museum has a fine collection of objects from prehistoric to Roman and Moorish times.

✉ Plaza Jerónimo Páez 7 ☎ 957 47 40 11 🕐 Wed–Sat 9–8.30, Tue 2.30–8.30, Sun 9–2.30 Inexpensive; free to EU citizens

MUSEO DE BELLAS ARTES

This fine arts museum contains paintings and sculptures by some of Spain's great masters including Goya, Luis Maroles and Alonso.

✉ Plaza de Potro, 1 ☎ 957 47 33 45 🕐 Wed–Sat 9–8.30, Tue 2.30–8.30 Sun 9–2.30 Inexpensive; free to EU citizens

MUSEO MUNICIPAL TAURINO

The Municipal Bullfighting Museum, which is housed in an elegant 16th-century mansion, has an unusual and fascinating display of items and memorabilia relating to some of Córdoba's most famous bullfighters, including the legendary Manolete.

Plaza Maimónides 5 957 20 10 56 Tue–Sat 10–2, 4.30–6.30, Sun and public hols 9.30–2.30 Inexpensive; free Fri

PALACIO DE VIANA

The Viana Palace warrants a visit, if only to see the beautiful patios and gardens of this fine 15th-century building. There are collections of paintings, porcelain, furniture and tapestries worth seeing. Note the splendid Mudéjar ceiling above the stairway to the first floor. Visitors are given a one-hour guided tour.

Rejas de Don Gome 2 957 49 67 41 Oct–May Mon–Fri 10–1, 4–6, Sat 10–1; mid-Jun to Sep 9–2; closed 1–15 Jun, Sun, public hols Inexpensive

TORRE DE LA CALAHORRA

Housed in the 14th-century Moorish fortress across the river, the Museo Histórico (Córdoba City Museum) makes clever use of multi-vision presentations to trace the history of Córdoba at the height of its golden era.

Puente Romano 957 29 39 29 Daily 10–6 Inexpensive

ESTEPONA

Some 36km (22 miles) west of Marbella is Estepona, another of the Costa del Sol's fast-developing resorts. It offers the attractions of a long beach, pleasant seafront promenade, a marina and at least three golf courses. It is also a good base for sailing and windsurfing. This former fishing village retains a large fleet protected by a harbour which also has moorings for some 400 yachts and pleasure craft. An enjoyable pastime is to wander down to the port early in the morning and watch the fresh catch being sold at the fish market.

The old town dates back to Roman and Moorish times. The focal point is the charming little square of the Plaza de las Flores, entered by four archways of trees. Amid trim orange trees and tropical plants, this is a good place in which to linger over a drink. The surrounding area offers a pleasant stroll through narrow streets lined with picturesque houses. Take a look at the church on Plaza de la Roloj and go down the steps to the Mercado Municipal, a covered market for fruit, vegetables and fresh fish. Above the little town are old castle ruins.

www.estepona.es

121 D5 82km (51 miles) west of Málaga

Many restaurants and bars (€–€€€) Fiesta de San Isidro (15 May); local festival (early Jul); Fiesta de Virgen del Carmen (16 Jul)

Avenida San Lorenzo 1 952 80 09 13/20 02

FUENGIROLA

Some 9km (5.5 miles) west of Benalmádena Costa is the prominent resort of Fuengirola, once a peaceful little fishing village. Now the scene is one of solid high-rise apartment blocks and buildings. The old part of the town, however, presents another side of Fuengirola. A lively meeting place is the Plaza de la Constitución, which is dominated by Fuengirola's main church. The old fishermen's district of Santa Fé has plenty of character and high above the town is the old Moorish Castle, Castillo de Sohail.

The castle, which is thought to have originated with the Romans, was rebuilt by the Moors and destroyed in the 15th century during the Christian reconquest. The present structure dates from 1730 and is open to the public. A walk up here is also recommended for the excellent coastal views.

Fuengirola is popular with northern Europeans who come for extended stays in the winter. There are many English-run bars and souvenir shops here and in neighbouring Los Boliches. The summer season is always lively; the long sweep of beach appeals to families. Fuengirola has several other attractions geared to children, such as the small zoo, an Aquapark at nearby Mijas Costa and the ever-popular Tivoli World up the road.

Water sports are on offer and the resort has an attractive yacht club and marina, along with an extended promenade, the Paseo Marítimo linking Fuengirola, Los Boliches, and Carvajal, which has so far retained a more Spanish feel and has a lovely beach.

www.fuengirola.org

123 D7 29km (18 miles) west of Málaga Many restaurants (€–€€€) Corner Avenida Ramón y Cajal and Calle Alfonso XIII RENFE station at Avenida Jesús Santos Rein (half-hourly service to Málaga)

Paseo Jesús Santos Rein 6 952 46 74 57

GAUCÍN

About 40 minutes away from the coast between Casares and Ronda, Gaucín is yet another of those enchanting little white towns you come across while travelling around the Andalucían countryside. As you approach you will encounter a cluster of whitewashed houses, topped by red roofs, spread out beneath the rocks.

The old Moorish fortress, Castillo de Aguila (Eagle's Castle), now partly restored, stands high above the village, forming a silhouette against the backdrop of mountains. From this vantage point there are magnificent views across the valley of the Guadiaro River, reaching out to the coastline as far as the Rock of Gibraltar.

The village is delightful and is filled with flowers and plants. Its narrow streets and one-way system are not conducive to driving,

however, and the place is best explored on foot. The daily fish market is always a lively event.

Gaucín makes a good base from which to explore the hinterland, which is dotted about with attractive towns and villages such as Ronda, Grazalema, Casares, Ubrique and Jimena de la Frontera.

121 D5 · 120km (75 miles) west of Málaga · Several restaurants · Local bus services · Romería San Juan (23 Jun); Fería Virgen de las Nieves (second week Aug); Fiesta de Santo Niño (8, 9 and 10 Sep) · Calle Fuente 91, Casares · 952 89 41 26

LA GIRALDA Y LA CATEDRAL, SEVILLA

See pages 32–33.

Marbella

Marbella is synonymous with the hedonistic world of the jet set. Since its meteoric rise to fame, Marbella has indeed never ceased to set itself above its fellow resorts along the coast, by continuing to cultivate its image as a playground of the rich and famous with their luxury yachts and glamorous lifestyles.

Marbella's development can be traced back to the 1940s, with the founding of the El Rodeo restaurant and inn by the Spanish aristocrat Ricardo Soriano. His nephew, Prince Alfonso Hohenlohe of Liechtenstein, went on to develop a small beach property into the Marbella Club chalet complex for his friends among the international set. This continued to attract celebrities to the area and led to the construction of a string of luxurious hotels which were built along the coast on either side of Marbella town, offering beautiful gardens, pools and sports facilities.

After the halcyon days of the 1970s and early '80s, there was an economic slump. Marbella went into a decline and began to wane in popularity. Then in the early 1990s, ambitious programmes were put forward to give the resort a much needed facelift. The remodelling of the Paseo Marítimo, the planting of palms and beautifying of the beaches, along with the construction of sorely needed underground parking areas and pledges to clean the place up in general, did much to restore Marbella's image and prestige. Marbella continues to prosper and grow. Urban developments spread out in all directions, while more projects are underway to propagate the image of the 'New Marbella'.

There are several Marbellas – the town itself, now a busy commercial hub, the beachfront and marina, and its picturesque old quarter, the Casco Antiguo (Old Town) (► 28–29). In the heart of Marbella town there are plush apartments overlooking the sea. From the Casco Antiguo a short walk will take you to the Parque de la Alameda (Alameda Park). The pleasant little park features exotic plants, trees and fountains, with attractively tiled benches adding to the scene. Stroll down to the beachfront through the Avenida del Mar, a broad pedestrian-only avenue adorned with flowers and trees and a series of lively Salvador Dalí sculptures.

The Paseo Marítimo, which stretches far on either side of town, offers an enjoyable seafront stroll, with bars and restaurants lining the route. Many improvements have been made to the long stretch of beach, shaded at regular intervals by palm trees. Have a

wander around the Puerto Deportivo (yacht harbour), where you can linger over a drink or a meal.

Two museums (in and around the Old Town) are worth a visit; the **Museo Bonsai,** for its delightful collection of Japanese-style minature trees, and the **Museo del Grabado Español Contemporáneo** (Museum of Spanish Contemporary Prints), for its exhibitions, which include works by prominent Spanish artists.

The municipality of Marbella covers a 28km (17-mile) stretch of coastline, which extends from the marina and the residential area of Cabo Pino, east of the town, to Guadalmina out to the west. The section from Marbella to Guadalmina has come to be known as the Golden Mile, so named for the concentration of luxurious hotels, restaurants and golf courses to be found here. Expensive villas with pools, set amid gardens of lush, tropical vegetation, complete the picture.

References to the 'exclusive resort of Marbella' can be misleading as, more often than not, the term applies not to the town, but to the hotels strung out on either side, including the plush Guadalmina development and the Puerto Banús

marina. This area is, in effect, the 'playground' of the jet set.

Puerto Banús (➤ 40–41) is officially part of San Pedro de Alcántara (➤ 82–83, located 3km/2 miles away) and is usually listed under Nueva Andalucía. However, it is within the community of Marbella and tends to be included in references to the town. It continues to be a place of pure enjoyment and a magnet for yachties. The marina has berths for over 900 and attracts craft of all sizes; millionaires' yachts are a common sight. There are also facilities for many water sports.

Marbella continues to attract the celebrities and stars. The partying goes on but has become less visible as more of the social scene takes place privately.

www.turismomarbella.com

121 D6 56km (35 miles) west of Málaga Wide range of restaurants, many (€€€) Bus station, Avenida del Trapiche, s/n 952 76 44 00. Avenida Ricardo Soriano for local services Carnival (pre-Lent), Fería de la Virgen del Carmen (16 Jul), Fería de San Bernabé Patrón (Jun), Fería de San Pedro (Oct)

Glorieta de la Fontanilla, Paseo Marítimo 952 77 14 42; Plaza de los Naranjos 952 82 35 50

Arco de Marbello

CN-340, Km 183.5 952 82 28 18

Museo Bonsai

Parque Arroyo de la Represa 952 86 29 26 Daily 10–1.30, 4.30–8 Avenida Ricardo Soriano Inexpensive

Museo del Grabado Español Contemporáneo

Hospital Bazán, s/n 952 82 50 35 Mon–Fri 10–2, 5.30–8.30, Sun 10–2 Avenida Ricardo Soriano

MARBELLA'S CASCO ANTIGUO

See pages 28–29.

LA MEZQUITA, CÓRDOBA

See pages 34–35.

MIJAS

See pages 36–37.

PUERTO BANÚS

See pages 40–41.

RONDA

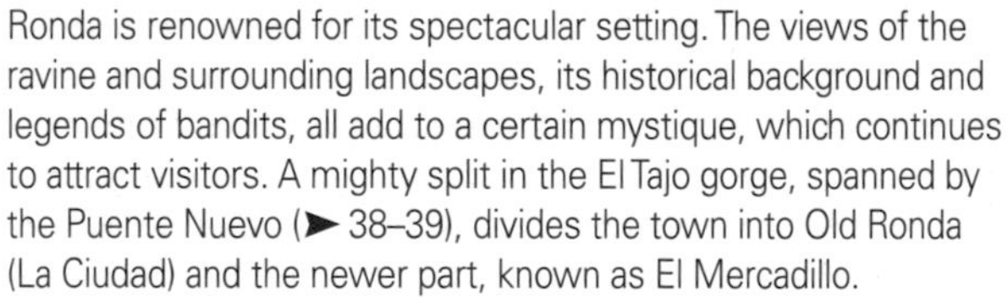

Ronda is renowned for its spectacular setting. The views of the ravine and surrounding landscapes, its historical background and legends of bandits, all add to a certain mystique, which continues to attract visitors. A mighty split in the El Tajo gorge, spanned by the Puente Nuevo (➤ 38–39), divides the town into Old Ronda (La Ciudad) and the newer part, known as El Mercadillo.

Most monuments of note are in the old town, which retains Moorish influences. These include the imposing Church of Santa Maria la Mayor, the Minaret of San Sebastian, the Palacio de Mondragón and the Casa del Gigante, the Palacio del Marqués de Salvatierra and the gardens of the Casa del Rey Moro. The Museo Lara (Science and History) and Museo del Bandolero (History and Legends of local bandits) are also worth a visit. The café-lined Plaza del Socorro is the focal point of the newer part of town, Ronda's main shopping centre, with more magnificent views from the attractive gardens of the Alameda del Tajo nearby.

Ronda has long-standing associations with bullfighting. The bullring, near the Puente Nuevo, was built in 1785 and is Spain's oldest. It was here that the rules of modern bullfighting were laid down by Francisco Romero, whose grandson Pedro Romero became one of Spain's most famous matadors. The bullring, now owned by Antonio Ordoñez, another of the greats, is used only for special fiestas. The bullfighting museum behind the ring contains glittering costumes, gear and photographs.

Ronda is a city with a romantic past. Two famous Americans, writer Ernest Hemingway and actor Orson Welles, were keen followers of the bullfight. Both spent much time here and each of them formed a close friendship with Ordoñez. By his request, Welles' ashes are scattered over the bulfighter's nearby ranch.

Some 20km (12.5 miles) southwest of Ronda is the **Cueva de la Pileta** (Pileta Cave), which has significant prehistoric rock paintings of animals, outlined in black and red, believed to date back over 25,000 years.

121 C6 118km (73 miles) northwest of Málaga Many restuarants (€–€€€) Buses from Algeciras, Málaga (via Bobadilla) Pedro Romero Festival (► 11)

Plaza de España 1 952 18 71 19; www.turismo deronda.es

Cueva de la Pileta

20km (12 miles) southwest of Ronda 952 16 73 43 Daily 10–1, 4–6; tours last about one hour Inexpensive

a walk in and around Ronda

This walk starts in the Plaza de España and takes you across the bridge to explore the old town of Ronda.

From the Plaza de España walk towards the Puente Nuevo (New Bridge).

Take a walk around the *parador*, on your right, for spectacular views of the gorge.

Return and cross over the bridge.

Look down into the ravine as you pass. A right turn down

Calle Tenorio will take you into a network of narrow streets and neat white houses to the Plaza del Campillo.

Keep walking and at the far end look for steps leading down the hill.

A short walk down reveals Ronda's houses perched on the clifftop. A further walk down will provide you with the classic view of the bridge, but it's a long climb up!

Back up again take the small street ahead to the Plaza Mondragón.

On the right is the Palacio de Mondragón, which was once a Moorish palace.

Continue to the Plaza de la Duquesa de Parcént. A left turn leads to the entrance of the Colegiata de Santa María la Mayor. Take the short slope down to Calle Armiñian and turn left. Note the Minaret of San Sebastian before crossing over to turn sharp right.

There are fine carvings on the façade of the Palacio del Marqués de Salvatierra (closed to the public).

Climb up Calle Santo Domingo to the Casa del Rey Moro, where you can take a long winding staircase down to the river and back up again to the gardens. Rejoin Calle Armiñán and cross back over the bridge to the Plaza de España.

Distance 4km (2.5 miles)
Time 2–3 hours
Start/end point Plaza de España 121 C6
Lunch Pedro Romero (€€) Virgen de la Paz 18, Ronda
952 87 11 10

RONDA'S PUENTE NUEVO

See pages 38–39.

SAN PEDRO DE ALCÁNTARA

San Pedro de Alcántara has undergone a facelift in recent years, with pleasing results. A development programme incorporating a new coastal promenade and beach improvements, stretching from Puerto Banús to Guadalmina, has given it a boost as an increasingly popular resort.

On the northern side of the coastal road is the small town itself, which has a neat, pleasant appearance. The Calle Marqués del Duero, attractively shaded by orange trees and palms, and lined with shops and cafés, leads up the hill to the small square of Plaza de la Iglesia adorned by a fountain. Adjacent to the town hall is San Pedro's parish church. Its white façade framed by two palm trees makes an attractive picture.

San Pedro is the first centre in Spain to have introduced the sport of cable skiing, which involves the water skier being towed by cable for long distances.

Three archaeological sites in the vicinity are worth exploring: the sixth-century Visigoth Basílica de Vega del Mar, the Villa Romana de Río Verde, remnants of a Roman villa from the first century, and Las Bovedas, where the remains of old Roman thermal baths can be seen.

121 D6 70km (43 miles) west of Málaga Choice of restaurants and bars (€–€€€) Avenida Marques del Duero, 69 952 78 52 52

SAN ROQUE/SOTOGRANDE

This is the place for big-time golfers and is said to have Spain's highest proportion of registered golfers in any one centre. Among the four golf courses, the Valderrama Robert Trent Jones Course played host to the 1997 Ryder Cup. Polo is also played here during the summer and the Sotogrande Marina is another attraction.

The small town is an attractive base in itself with narrow streets and plenty of flowers and plants. The lively cafés and restaurants of the Campamento area appeal to a younger crowd.

120 E4 100km (62 miles) west of Málaga Wide choice Bus connections San Roque Annual Fair (early Sep); Sotogrande golf tournaments, polo matches (Jul, Aug, Sep) Avenida 20 Abril, s/n, La Línea 956 76 99 50

Sevilla

Sevilla is the capital of Andalucía and Spain's fourth largest city. It is dominated by La Giralda and the great cathedral that this minaret tower adjoins (► 32–33). Various cultures have left their mark here, from the Romans to the Moors and the Christians. An early carving on the Jerez Gate alludes to the legendary origins of the city: 'Hercules built me, Caesar surrounded me with walls and towers, the King Saint took me.'

Sevilla is believed to have been founded by the Iberians. Subsequent occupiers included the Greeks, Phoenicians and the Carthaginians (who named it Hispalis). Around 205BC the town was taken over by the Romans and it continued to flourish under Julius Caesar. During the fifth century it became the capital of the Visigoths. It was captured in AD712 by the Moors, whose long occupation has left magnificent traces of their artistic merits.

In 1248 Sevilla was reconquered by Ferdinand III of Castille. But it was the discovery of America that brought prosperity to Sevilla, when Columbus returned here from his first voyage in 1493. In the 16th and 17th centuries the port became the most important in Spain. During this period, the Sevilla school of painters brought great prestige to the city.

Sevilla is a city to explore on foot with the cathedral a good focal point from which to start. The medieval quarter of the Barrio Santa Cruz is a delightful maze of narrow streets and whitewashed houses adorned with wrought-iron balconies decked with flowers.

A stroll around town reveals mansions, squares and lovely parks, such as the Parque de Maria Luisa, the Murillo gardens and those of the Reales Alcazares. The large Plaza de España contains a tiny canal, decorated bridges and fountains. Over the bridge is the Triana area. Alternative ways of getting around are by 'SevillaTour' buses or with style in a horse-drawn carriage.

www.turismosevilla.org

116 C4 219km (136 miles) northwest of Málaga Huge choice of restaurants and *tapas* bars Bus stations: Prado de San Sebastían (954 41 71 11); Plaza de Armas (954 90 77 37) Estación de FFCC Santa Justa, Avenida Kansas City, s/n (954 54 02 02) Semana Santa (Easter), Fería de Sevilla (2 weeks after Easter), Corpus Christi, Fiesta de la Virgen de los Reyes (15 Aug) Avenida de la Constitucíon 21 B 954 22 14 04

WHAT TO SEE IN SEVILLA

CASA DE PILATOS

This 16th-century private mansion is one of Sevilla's jewels. Combining Mudéjar, Gothic and Renaissance styles, its patios, archways and salons are adorned with delicate carving, tilework and wooden coffered ceilings. A grand staircase leads to the upper floors, which contain a collection of art. The adjoining gardens may also be visited.

Plaza Pilatos 1 954 22 52 98 Daily 9–6 C1, C2, C3, C4 Inexpensive; free Tue pm

MUSEO ARQUEOLÓGICO

Housed in the Renaissance palace built for the 1929 Ibero-America Exhibition, the Archeological Museum has a fine collection of objects from prehistory and the Moorish culture. Outstanding among its exhibits is the Carombolo Treasure; from the seventh century, this includes jewellery from the Tartessos civilization.

Plaza de América 954 23 24 01 Wed–Sat 9–8, Tue 3–8, Sun, public hols 9–2 Inexpensive; free to EU citizens

MUSEO DE BELLAS ARTES

Housed in the former Convento de la Merced, the museum contains a splendid collection of fine art with paintings and sculpture, ceramics and weapons. Room V contains works of art by some of the great Spanish masters, including Zurbarán and Murillo.

Plaza de América 954 23 24 01 Wed–Sat 9–8, Tue 3–8, Sun, public hols 9–2 Inexpensive; free to EU citizens

REALES ALCÁZARES

Former Moorish palaces, largely rebuilt for Christian kings after the reconquest of Sevilla: the centrepiece, Palacio Mudéjar del Rey Don Pedro, built by Pedro I in the 14th century, is a superb example of Mudéjar art. Salons, archways and columns are richly decorated with exquisite carvings, ceramics and wooden ceilings. Note the domed ceiling of the Salón de Embajadores (Hall of Ambassadors).

Plaza del Triunfo 954 50 23 23 Tue–Sat 9:30–7, Sun 9:30–5 Moderate C1, C2, C3, C4 Go early if possible. Restrictions on numbers allowed in during busy periods can result in queues

TARIFA

To stand on the Punta de Tarifa is to be at the southernmost point of Europe, with the coast of the African continent only 14km (9 miles) away. Situated on the fringe of the Costa del Sol, Tarifa has a totally different atmosphere about it which in itself makes a visit worthwhile.

The town has played an important role in the history of the Iberian Peninsula. It was named after Tarif Ibn Malik, the Moorish leader who in AD710 arrived here from North Africa with a small band of men and took possession of the area. This led to the larger invasion which took place the following year and the subsequent Moorish conquest of most of present-day Spain. Tarifa was taken by the Christians in 1292 but the siege was maintained for the next couple of years.

Entrance to the town, which is encircled by walls, is through a Moorish gate. With its dazzling white houses and maze of narrow, winding streets, Tarifa retains a distinctive Moorish look. The port offers a good view of the old Moorish castle above the town, which is in the hands of the Spanish Navy and not open to the public.

Tarifa has a long expanse of sandy beach backed by pine trees. This marks the meeting point of the Mediterranean and the Atlantic and the strong winds that sweep across the sand create excellent conditions for windsurfing in the bay. The place has now become a top centre for the sport, with kitesurfing also fast gaining in popularity.

www.tarifaweb.com

120 F3 21km (13 miles) west of Algeciras Choice of restaurants (€–€€€) Bus connections with Algeciras Día de los Reyes (6 Jan); Carnival (pre-Lent); Romería del Consejo (15 May); Fiesta de San Juan (24 Jun); Fiesta de la Virgen del Carmen (16 Jul); National Folk Music Festival (early Aug); Fiesta de Nuestra Señora de la Luz (early Sep)

Paseo de la Alameda 956 68 09 93

GRUPO ESCOLAR DE NIÑOS
MIGUEL DE CERVANTES

a drive to Antequera

This drive offers striking scenery, taking you first to Antequera and continuing to the bizarre rock formations in the El Torcal National Park.

From Torremolinos turn onto the N340 towards Málaga. Passing the airport on your left, continue on the Málaga ring road (Ronda de Málaga) and follow the signs to Antequera (N331).

After the turn off to Finca de la Concepción, this excellent highway climbs up through the hills of the Montes de Málaga, scattered with olive groves and tiny white houses. As you approach Antequera dramatic rock shapes rise from the fertile plains, noticeably the striking form of the so-called Peña de los Enamorados (Lovers' Rock). About an hour after departure you should enter Antequera (➤ 60–61). Allow time to explore this attractive city of churches and convents.

Take the Calle de la Legión in a southerly direction and a few moments out of town pause to admire the magnificent views of Antequera on your left, backed by the distinctive form of the Peña de los Enamorados. Take the C3310, following the signs to Torcal.

The road winds through a barren landscape of rocks and boulders for about half an hour before reaching a right turn to Parque Natural del Torcal de Antequera. As you drive through the park, the shapes become increasingly curious, until the whole landscape appears positively lunar-like. The road ends about 15 minutes later by a small hut; walking trails start from here.

Rejoin the C3310 and continue south to the coast and return to Torremolinos.

Distance 125km (77.5 miles)
Time About 6 hours
Start/end point Torremolinos ✚ 121 D8
Lunch Parador de Antequera (€€) ✉ García del Olmo, Antequera
☎ 952 84 02 61

TORREMOLINOS

Torremolinos, lying only 8km (5 miles) west of Málaga airport, heralds the start of the most developed part of the coast. To many, this stretch of coast, lined with high-rise apartment blocks and development as far as Estepona, represents the real Costa del Sol.

Torremolinos began to grow as a holiday resort in the 1950s, when the building of luxury hotels got under way, and it became one of the first places on this coast to cater for mass tourism. Its proximity to Málaga airport is a point in its favour. At the height of summer the resort has a great appeal for the younger set, with a reputation for its hectic night life. Out of season, however, it takes on a different mantle. The pace slows down and, at weekends in particular, the city appears almost like a suburb, with Spanish families much in evidence.

There's a definite divide between the town and the beach area below. The main artery of the town is the pedestrian-only Calle San Miguel. Lined with a varied assortment of shops and surrounded by numerous bars and restaurants, this mini *ramblas* attracts a constant flow of people. Other popular spots for eating and drinking are the small Andalucían-style development of Pueblo Blanco nearby, and the area of El Calvario, beyond the top end of San Miguel. A favourite establishment here is the Galloping Major (splendidly translated as El Comandante Galopando), which opened in 1964 as the first English-style pub in Torremolinos.

At the south end of San Miguel the Cuesta del Tajo leads down winding steps filled with souvenir shops to the El Bajondillo beach.

The beach area shows another side of Torremolinos. With massive hotels, apartment blocks, bars and restaurants, this area is packed during the summer. To the left, the Playa de Bajondillo gives way to the beaches of Playamar and Los Alamos. To the right, beyond the Castillo de Santa Clara, lie the beach areas of La Carihuela and Montemar.

The Paseo Marítimo, the seafront promenade, extends east to Playamar and west to La Carihuela, now continuing as far as

Benalmádena Costa. The walk to La Carihuela offers pleasant sea views and some dramatic rock formations, before entering the old fishing village of La Carihuela, which is a delightful area of picturesque little houses and streets. It has a good reputation for excellent fish and seafood restaurants. In summer, the *chiringuitos* (beach bars) are well worth sampling.

A pioneer of the development of Torremolinos was an Englishman. George Langworthy (Don Jorge or El Señor Inglés as he was called by the local people) made history when in 1930 he opened up his home, the Hacienda Santa Clara, as a residence for foreigners, creating a centre for the needy. He grew to be held in great esteem by the local people and, after his death, a street was named for him and a monument erected in his honour.

www.ayto-torremolinos.org

121 D8 12km (7.5 miles) west of Málaga Many pubs, restaurants, bars (€–€€€) Half-hourly to Málaga (25 minutes) and Fuengirola

Carnival (pre-Lent); Feria de Verdiales (Mar); Easter; Fiesta de la Virgen del Carmen (16 Jul); Día del Turista (early Sep); Feria de San Miguel (late Sep); Romería de San Miguel (Sun, late Sep)

Main office: Plaza Blas Infante 1 (952 37 95 12); Plaza de la Independencia, s/n (952 37 42 31); Playa de Bajondillo (952 37 19 09)

East of Málaga

Less developed than western Málaga, this stretch of Mediterranean shoreline has a more rocky appearance, a number of pleasant beaches and attractive resorts such as Nerja. There is an appealing freshness to Nerja's old town of narrow streets, and the limestone Cuevas de Nerja are only 4km (2.5 miles) east.

Beyond the coast you will discover the essence of Andalucía among great mountain ranges, with the Sierra Nevada at the heart and the world-famous buildings of Granada which embodies Spain's Moorish past in its architectural treasures. The variety of the landscape and the charm and individuality of the people will reward those visitors who are searching for the heart and soul of southern Spain.

ALMUÑÉCAR

Almuñécar, situated in the province of Granada, within the coastline now designated as the Costa Tropical, lies amid orchards of tropical fruits. It presents a very picturesque scene, typical of so many villages to be found in southern Spain, with a cluster of whitewashed houses rising up the hillside crowned by an old castle. Its history goes back to the time of the Phoenicians, with subsequent occupation by the Romans and the Moors. The Castillo de San Miguel stands on top of a tall rock, dividing two bays. It was built during the reign of Carlos V, over the site of a former Moorish fortress, and features a great square tower known as La Mazmorra.

The town itself is a jumble of narrow, cobblestoned streets, climbing steeply up to the summit. Do not miss a visit to the Ornithological Park located at the foot of the hill. Here you can see brilliantly coloured parrots and rare species of birds in a beautiful setting of subtropical plants and flowers. The seafront is lined with apartment blocks, bars and restaurants, with a lively scene by day and night during the season.

Also worth a visit is the small archaeological museum housed in the Cueva de los Siete Palacios, thought to have been a Roman reservoir for water. The museum has a display of objects from the area (Tue–Sat 11–2 and 6–8).

A look-out post at nearby Punta de la Mona offers sweeping views of the harbour and the Mediterranean.

123 E6 84km (52 miles) east of Málaga Variety of restaurants Local bus services
Avenida Europa-Palacete La Najarra 958 63 11 25

CÓMPETA

Way up in the mountains of La Axarquiá, the region east of Málaga, is the small town of Cómpeta, which can be reached by taking the road leading inland from Torrox-Costa.

Cómpeta is noted for its attractive setting, perched atop a mountain ridge surrounded by vineyards. It is one of a number of easily accessible Andalucían towns and villages located in the hills which offer fine views down to the coast. The town is made up of a cluster of whitewashed houses and winding streets. On the main square stands the baroque Iglesia de la Asunción, which has an impressive bell tower.

Cómpeta has a sizeable community of foreign residents, a number of whom are involved with craft industries. A big attraction is the lively wine festival which is held each year in August in the main square.

123 D5 51km (31.5 miles) east of Málaga Several restaurants (€–€€) Local services Noche del Vino (15 Aug)
Plaza Almijira s/n 952 55 33 01

CUEVAS DE NERJA

See pages 30–31.

FRIGILIANA

It is well worth taking a short drive of some 6km (4 miles) up into the hills from Nerja to visit Frigiliana. This pretty little village spreads its dazzlingly whitewashed houses out over the hills in two sections. The older part is a mass of narrow, cobbled streets winding their way up the hillside with wonderful views over fertile orchards and the coast. Here and there you may come across a donkey patiently carrying its load. Streets and balconies are decked out with flowers. The village continues to attract a growing

number of visitors, with more shops and restaurants springing up all over.

One of the last battles between the Christians and the Moors was fought in the area in the 16th century, resulting in victory for the Christians. The tale of this glorious event is related by way of a series of ceramic tiles on the walls of the houses.

123 D6 56km (35 miles) east of Málaga Some restaurants (€€) Local Día de la Cruz (3 May); Fería de San Antonio (13 Jun) Plaza del Ingenio, s/n 952 53 31 26

FUENTE VAQUEROS

Fuente Vaqueros is home to the **Casa Museo García Lorca**. The museum was the former home of the poet and playwright Federico García Lorca, who was born in Fuente Vaqueros in 1898. Lorca, who spent much time in nearby Granada, became known for the sensitivity of his poetry and the powerful drama of his plays, such as *Yerma*, *Blood Wedding* and *The House of Bernarda Alba*, which continue to be widely produced on stage throughout the world. He was assassinated near Viznar during the Spanish Civil War.

123 C7 17km (10.5 miles) west of Granada

Casa Museo Federico García Lorca

Calle Poeta García Lorca, 4 958 51 64 53; www.museogarcialorca.org Tue–Sun 10–1, 4–8 (winter 4–6). Tours hourly Inexpensive

Granada

Granada is the capital of its province, the seat of an archbishop and a university town. In addition to La Alhambra, with which Granada is so closely associated, the city has much else to commend it: its beautiful setting, built on three hills backed by the snowy peaks of the Sierra Nevada, its historic links with the past and significant religious festivals. A visit to Granada could be made from the coast within a day. However, more time is recommended to explore one of Spain's crowning glories, the last kingdom of the Moors.

Known as Iliberis during the Iberian culture, Granada was taken by the Romans and the Visigoths before its conquest by the Moors in 711. The 11th century saw the decline of the Caliphate of Córdoba and the beginning of the Kingdom of Granada. From the 13th century, until its downfall at the end of the 15th century, Granada flourished as a prosperous cultural centre with the construction of magnificent buildings such as La Alhambra (➤ 24–25). In 1492 Granada was taken by the Catholic Monarchs. This marked the end of Moorish rule and Spain's history was changed. Granada continued to prosper during the Renaissance but declined after the repression of a Moorish uprising in the 16th century.

The priority for most visitors is the palace of La Alhambra. Magical as this Moorish palace is, it is surrounded by some equally fascinating places. The summer palace of El Generalife, with its shady avenues, water gardens, fountains and airy gazebos, is a neighbour of La Alhambra that you really should visit. On the slopes of the hill facing La Alhambra is the picturesque old Moorish quarter of Albaicín, a labyrinth of steep, narrow streets and small squares that has changed little with time. To the east rises the hill of Sacramonte, formerly the home of cave-dwelling gypsies.

www.turismodegranada.es

123 C7 129km (80 miles) northeast of Málaga Variety of bars and restaurants (€–€€€) Estación de Autobuses, Ctra de Jaén s/n 958 18 54 80/98 Estación de FFCC, Avenida de Andalucía s/n 958 20 40 00 Día de la Toma (1, 2 Jan); Semana Santa (Easter); Corpus Christi, International Music and Dance Festival (end Jun, early Jul); Romería (29 Sep); International Jazz Festival (Nov)

Corral del Carbón, Plaza de Mariana Pineda, 10 Bajo 958 24 71 28

WHAT TO SEE IN GRANADA

CAPILLA REAL

The Royal Chapel, sanctioned by the Catholic Monarchs for their burial, was begun in 1506 and completed under the reign of Hapsburg Emperor Charles V in 1521. It has a richly adorned interior. In the chancel, closed by a screen, are the mausoleums of King Ferdinand and Queen Isabella, along with their daughter Juana la Loca and her husband Philip the Fair. A museum reached through the north arm of the transept displays items of historical interest and a fine collection of paintings and sculpture.

Oficios 3 (Cathedral) 958 22 78 48 Apr–Oct Mon–Sat 10.30–1, 4–7, Sun 11–1, 4–7 Inexpensive RENFE station Granada

CASA MANUEL DE FALLA

Manuel de Falla (1876–1946) was born in Cádiz and taught by Pedrell, the founder of Spain's modern national school of composition. He spent several years in Paris, but drew on his own native musical traditions in works such as the popular ballet music *The Three-Cornered Hat.* The composer lived in this house for a number of years. Items on display relate to his life.

Antequerela Alta 11 958 22 21 89 Tue–Sat 10–1.30
Inexpensive

CATEDRAL

The cathedral was begun in 1528 on the orders of the Catholic Monarchs. Construction was under the great master Diego de Siloé, and continued after his death in 1528. It features a magnificent Capilla Real (Royal Chapel) and has a notable rotunda, with some fine paintings by Alonso Cano, a native of Granada.

Gran Vía 5 958 22 29 59 Mon–Sat 10.30–1.30, 4–7, Sun 4–7
Inexpensive

MONASTERIO DE LA CARTUJA

This former Carthusian Monastery, which dates back to the 16th century, has a worthwhile collection of paintings and sculpture.

Paseo de la Cartuja, s/n 958 16 19 32 Mon–Sat 10–1, 4–6.30
Inexpensive (free Sun)

MUSEO ARQUEOLÓGICO

The museum is housed in the Casa Castril, an elegant Renaissance palace noted for its delicately carved plateresque doorway. It has a fine collection of ceramics from Roman and Moorish times, in addition to some superb Egyptian vases unearthed in the region.

Carrera del Darro 41 958 22 56 40
Wed–Sat 9–6, Tue 2.30–6, Sun 9–2.30 Inexpensive; free to EU citizens

NERJA

Nerja lies in a fertile valley of fruit orchards, known mainly for the production of peaches and pomegranates. Its attractive setting amid cliffs overlooking rocky coves has earned its reputation as the jewel of the eastern Costa del Sol. Its name is derived from the old Moorish word *naricha,* meaning 'rich in water'. The town began as a Moorish farming estate during the 10th century, a centre of the silk and sugar industries. All reminders of its Moorish past and much of Nerja were destroyed in the 1884 earthquake.

Nerja's famous promenade received its name when King Alfonso XII was touring the area to show sympathy following the earthquake on Christmas Day in 1884. While visiting the town he stood on the promontory, with its magnificent view of the Mediterranean, and declared it the Balcón de Europa (Balcony of Europe). The name stuck.

Nerja stands out as one of the most appealing of the resorts east of Málaga. It retains the charm of its old town with narrow streets, many pedestrian-only, and lined with whitewashed houses adorned with flowers and crammed with restaurants. These streets lead down to the Bálcon de Europa. A series of steps will take you down to the Paseo de los Caribineros and a walkway via several coves onto the popular Playa de Burriana.

Although Nerja has grown into a popular resort, it has managed to escape the sort of development found along much of its neighbouring western coastline. Most noticeably it has managed to retain its small-town atmosphere. Now linked to Málaga by the Autovía del Mediterraneo, expansion is inevitably on its way.

Some 4km (2.5 miles) east of Nerja lies Maro. Perched on a clifftop above a small cove, this pretty village offers good views of the coastline. Of particular interest is the attractive little Church of Nuestra Señora de las Maravillas de Maro, and the aqueduct.

www.nerja.org

123 D6 52km (32 miles) east of Málaga Choice of restaurants and bars (€–€€€) Bus connections Puerta del Mar 4 952 52 15 31

RINCÓN DE LA VICTORIA

Lying some 12km (7.5 miles) east of Málaga, Rincón de la Victoria is a fast-developing resort. It offers a pleasant new seafront promenade, some modest accommodation, an 18-hole golf course, riding, tennis and boats for hire. The resort has a reputation for good fish restaurants, a speciality being a small

sardine-type fish known as *victorianos*, and *coquinas* (clams). The Wednesday market is always a great event.

122 D4 12km (7.5 miles) east of Málaga

Fiesta de la Virgen del la Candelaria (1–3 Feb); Fiesta de la Virgen del Carmen (16 Jul); Fiesta de Verano (22–25 Aug)

Granada 2 B 952 40 77 68

SALOBREÑA

Some 13km (8 miles) east of Almuñécar is the attractive little town of Salobreña, within the stretch of coast now known as the Costa Tropical. It lies a short distance from the sea among fruit orchards and sugarcane plantations.

Salobreña consists of a cluster of whitewashed houses sprawling up the hill, dominated by the old Moorish *alcázar* known as El Capricho. The castle has been well restored and offers magnificent views of the coast, surrounding countryside and the beautiful peaks of the Sierra Nevada. Also worth a visit is the 16th century Church of Nuestra Señora del Rosario, which was built on the site of an old mosque.

Much of Salobreña's charm lies in the fact that it remains relatively unspoiled, with few hotels and restaurants. It provides a good gateway to Granada, however, and can receive quite an influx of visitors, especially at weekends. From here it is only 4km (2.5 miles) farther along the coast to Motril, principally known as a commercial centre for sugarcane. Take a look at the Sanctuary of Our Lady of the Head, which stands atop the hill. Enthusiasts can enjoy the golf course.

123 E7 93km (58 miles)east of Málaga Choice of restaurants (€–€€€) Bus connections Semana Santa (Easter): Fiesta de San Juan y San Pedro (end Jul); Fiesta de Nuestra Señora del Rosario (early Oct)

Plaza de Goya s/n 958 61 03 14

TORRE DEL MAR

Located in the eastern part of the Costa de Sol, Torre del Mar is the beach resort of Vélez-Málaga (➤ 182), capital of the Axarquiá region. There are unsubstantiated claims that Torre del Mar once formed part of an ancient Greek settlement known as Mainake, which is believed to have been destroyed by the Carthaginians, prior to the arrival of the Romans. These days the town consists primarily of a long beach lined with a string of high-rise apartment blocks catering mainly for summer visitors.

One of the resort's most pleasant features is the extended esplanade which follows the coast to the Marina of Caleta de Vélez. With over 200 berths, it presents an attractive scene of boats and yachts, offering sailing and a variety of other water sports. Its lively cafés and restaurants also provide a good place in which to idle the time away. Another bonus is the excellent seafood served here in numerous restaurants and bars.

123 D5 30km (18.5 miles) east of Málaga Choice of restaurants and bars (€–€€€) Bus connections Fiestas at Vélez-Málaga
Avenida de Andalucía 52 952 54 11 04

TORROX COSTA

Along the eastern end of the Costa del Sol, situated between Torre del Mar and Nerja, is the resort of Torrox Costa. Torrox consists basically of a long stretch of beach, backed with modern apartment blocks sympathetically designed to reflect Moorish architecture.

The resort has been developed primarily for summer visitors. The beach offers a number of water sports, while an extended promenade along the seafront has a reasonable choice of restaurants, bars and shops.

You might like to take a look at the Church of La Encarnación and the Hermitage of Nuestra Señora de las Nieves, both of which still retain traces of Moorish influences.

Scattered along the coast are a few old watchtowers and small fortresses, going back to the times when there was a threat of pirate invasion. Some 4km (2.5 miles) inland lies the old town of Torrox; built up the steep slopes of the hill, its whitewashed houses make an attractive pattern.

123 D5 47km (29 miles) east of Málaga · Choice of restaurants and bars (€–€€€) · Bus connections · Carnival (pre-Lent); La Cruz de Mayo (2 May); Fiesta de San Juan (23–24 Jun); Fiesta de la Virgen de la Nieves (5 Aug); local fair (4–7 Oct)

Centro Internacional, bloque 79 · 952 53 02 25

VÉLEZ-MÁLAGA

The small town of Vélez-Málaga lies 5km (3 miles) inland from Torre del Mar, surrounded by subtropical vegetation. Capital of La Axarquiá, it is the centre of an agricultural region known for its production of strawberries and its vineyards, which produce the muscatel grapes from which the famous Málaga wines are made. It is also a centre for the processing of olive oil and sugarcane. Ceramics feature among other industries. If you are here on a Thursday, take time to wander around its weekly market, always an enjoyable experience.

The town is crowned by a well-restored 13th-century Moorish castle. There are good views of the surrounding countryside from up here. The oldest part of the town, known as Arrabal de San Sebastián, is a picturesque area of narrow streets. You will also come across attractive mansions built during the 16th and 17th centuries. Of special note, among the several churches to be found in the town, is the 15th-century Church of Santa María la Mayor, which shows the Mudéjar style. This was the first building to be erected by the Christians following their victory over the Moors here in 1487.

123 D5 34km (21 miles) east of Málaga Many restaurants (€–€€€)
Bus connections
Avenida de Andalucia 119
952 54 11 04

ZUHEROS

The white houses of Zuheros cluster below a Moorish castle in the Sierra Subbética mountains, in a world of cliffs and rocky bluffs. A handsome church, the Inglesia de la Virgen de los Remedios, whose tower supplanted an earlier minaret, overlooks the main square, and a village museum displays objects from prehistoric, Roman and Moorish times. The narrow streets of Zuheros make for pleasant wandering, and are punctuated by fine viewpoints such as the Mirador de la Villa. East of the town is the Cueva de los Murcielagos (Cave of the Bats) with prehistoric paintings.

123 A5 · 60km (37 miles) southeast of Córdoba, entrance to town on the Baena road

Inciativas Subbéticas. c/Horno 50 · 957 69 47 75

Index

Acknowledgements

The Automobile Association would like to thank the following photographers, companies and picture libraries for their assistance in the preparation of this book.

Abbreviations for the picture credits are as follows – (t) top; (b) bottom; (c) centre; (l) left; (r) right; (AA) AA World Travel Library.

4l Car, AA/C Sawyer; **4c** La Alhambra in Granada, AA/D Robertson; **4r** Museo de Artes in Malaga, AA/J Poulsen; **5l** Man playing guitar, AA/M Chaplow; **5r** Flamenco show, AA/M Jourdan; **6/7** Car, AA/C Sawyer; **10** Horse drawn carriage, AA/A Molyneux; **12** Policeman, AA/J Edmanson; **12/13** Countryside in Jaen, AA/M Chaplow; **14** Donkeys, AA/J Tims; **14/15** Taxis, AA/A Molyneux; **16** Telephone AA/P Bennett; **20/21** La Alhambra in Granada, AA/D Robertson; **22/23** La Alcazaba in Granada, AA/M Chaplow; **23** View to La Alcazaba and Castillo de Gibralfaro in Malaga, AA/P Wilson; **24/25t** La Alhambra in Granada, AA/J Edmanson; **24/25b** La Alhambra, AA/J Edmanson; **26/27** Casares, AA/J Edmanson; **27** Casares. AA/J Tims; **28/29** Casco Antiguo in Marbella, AA/M Chaplow; **30** Cuevas de Nerja, AA/M Chaplow; **30/31** Cuevas de Nerja, AA/M Chaplow; **31** Cuevas de Nerja, AA/M Chaplow; **32** Seville, AA/M Chaplow; **32/33** Seville Cathedral, AA/P Wilson; **33** La Giralda, AA/P Wilson; **34/35** La Mezquita in Cordoba, AA/M Chaplow; **35t** La Mezquita in Cordoba, AA/M Chaplow; **35b** La Mezquita in Cordoba, AA/D Robertson; **36t** Jugs, AA/W Voysey; **36b** Mijas, AA/J Tims; **36/37** Mijas, AA/J Edmanson; **38** Puente Nuevo in Ronda, AA/P Wilson; **38/39** Puente Nuevo in Ronda, AA/P Wilson; **40** Marina at Puerto Banus, AA/J Edmanson; **40/41** Puerto Banus, AA/J Tims; **41** Puerto Banus, AA/M Chaplow; **42/43** Museo de Artes in Malaga, AA/J Poulsen; **45** Central Stadium in Malaga, AA/J Tims; **46/47** La Alcazaba, AA/P Wilson; **47** Castillo de Gibralfaro, AA/J Tims; **48/49** Plaza de la Constitucion, Malaga, AA/M Chaplow; **49** Plaza de la Merced in Malaga, AA/M Chaplow; **50** Malaga Cathedral, AA/J Tims; **51** Malaga Cathedral, AA/J Tims; **52/53** Malaga, AA/P Wilson; **54/55** Paseo del Parque, AA/M Chaplow; **56** Fish, Photodisc; **56/57** Façade in Malaga, AA/J Tims; **58** Hibiscus flower, AA/M Chaplow; **60** Antequera, AA/J Poulsen; **62/63** Antequera AA/J Tims; **64** Benalmadena, AA/J Tims; **65** Benalmadena, AA/J Tims; **66/67** Alcazar de Los Reyes Cristianos, AA/M Chaplow; **68/69** La Mezquita in Cordoba, AA/M Chaplow; **69** Coach driver in Cordoba, AA/D Robertson; **70/71** Estepona, AA/J Tims; **71** Plaza de la Constitucion in Fuengirola, AA/J Tims; **72/73** Guacin, AA/J Poulsen; **74** Marbella, AA/J Tims; **74/75** Beach in Marbella, AA/M Chaplow; **76/77** Beach in Marbella, AA/J Tims; 77 Marbella, AA/J Poulsen; 78 Bullring, AA/P Wilson; 78/9 Ronda, AA/J Edmanson; **80/81** Ronda, AA/M Chaplow; **82/83** San Roque, AA/J Tims; **83** San Pedro de Alcantara, AA/J Tims; **84/85** Seville, AA/D Robertson; **85** Shopkeeper, AA/A Molyneux; **86/87** Reales Alcazares, AA/A Molyneux; **88/89** Tarifa, AA/J Edmanson; **90/91** El Torcal National Park, AA/M Chaplow; **91** Antequera, AA/J Tims; **93** Torremolinos, AA/J Edmanson; **94t** Tourists in Torremolinos, AA/M Chaplow; **94b** Golf course in Torremolinos, AA/M Chaplow; **95** Frigiliana, AA/J Tims; **96** Almunecar, AA/J Tims; **97** Competa, AA/J Poulsen; **98/99** Frigiliana, AA/J Tims; **99** Sign in Frigiliana, AA/J Tims; **100/101** Granada, AA/J Edmanson; **102/103** Capilla Real, AA/D Robertson; **103** Granada, AA/M Chaplow; **105** Nerja, AA/J Tims; **106** Shrine at Rincon de la Victoria, AA/J Tims; **106/107** Salobrena, AA/J Tims; **108** Torre del Mar, AA/D Robertson; **109t** Torrox, AA/J Tims; **109b** Torrox, AA/J Tims; **110** Velez-Malaga, AA/J Tims; **110/111** Velez-Malaga AA/J Tims.

Every effort has been made to trace the copyright holders, and we apologise in advance for any accidental errors. We would be happy to apply the corrections in the following edition of this publication.

Maps

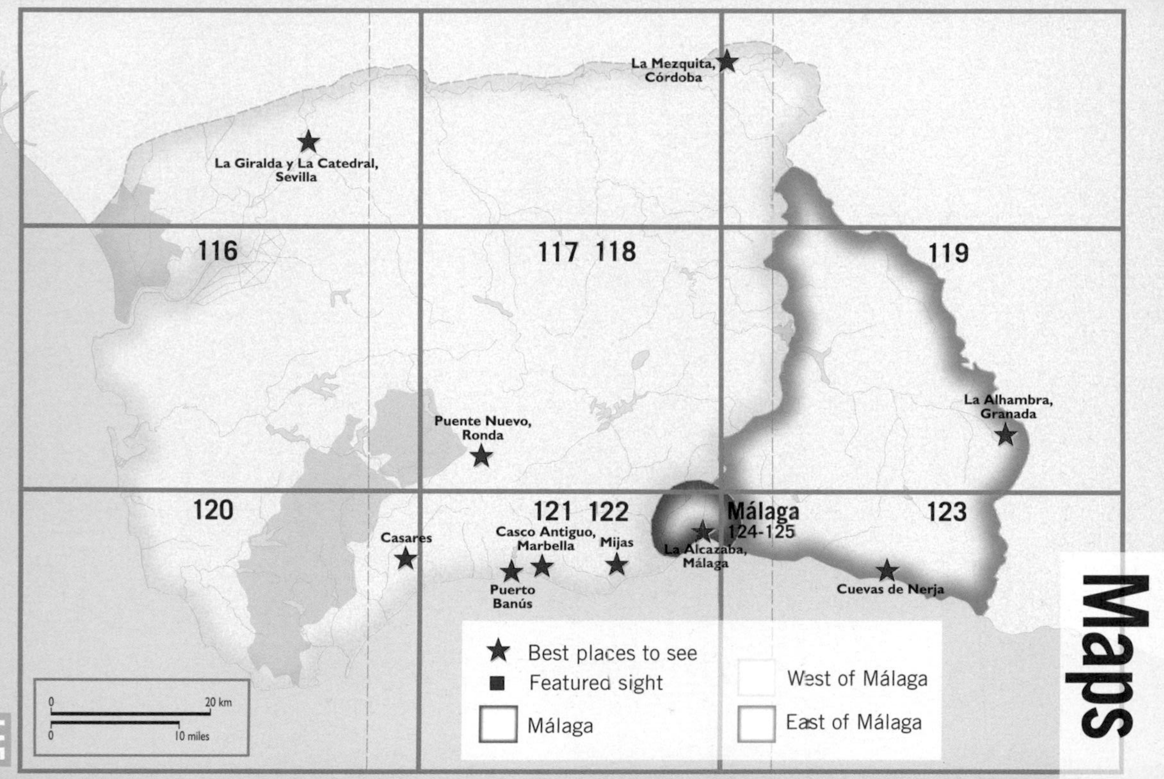

La Mezquita, Córdoba
La Giralda y La Catedral, Sevilla
116
117 118
119
La Alhambra, Granada
Puente Nuevo, Ronda
120
121 122
Málaga 124-125
123
Casares
Casco Antiguo, Marbella
Mijas
La Alcazaba, Málaga
Puerto Banús
Cuevas de Nerja
Best places to see
Featured sight
Málaga
West of Málaga
East of Málaga
0
20 km
0
10 miles

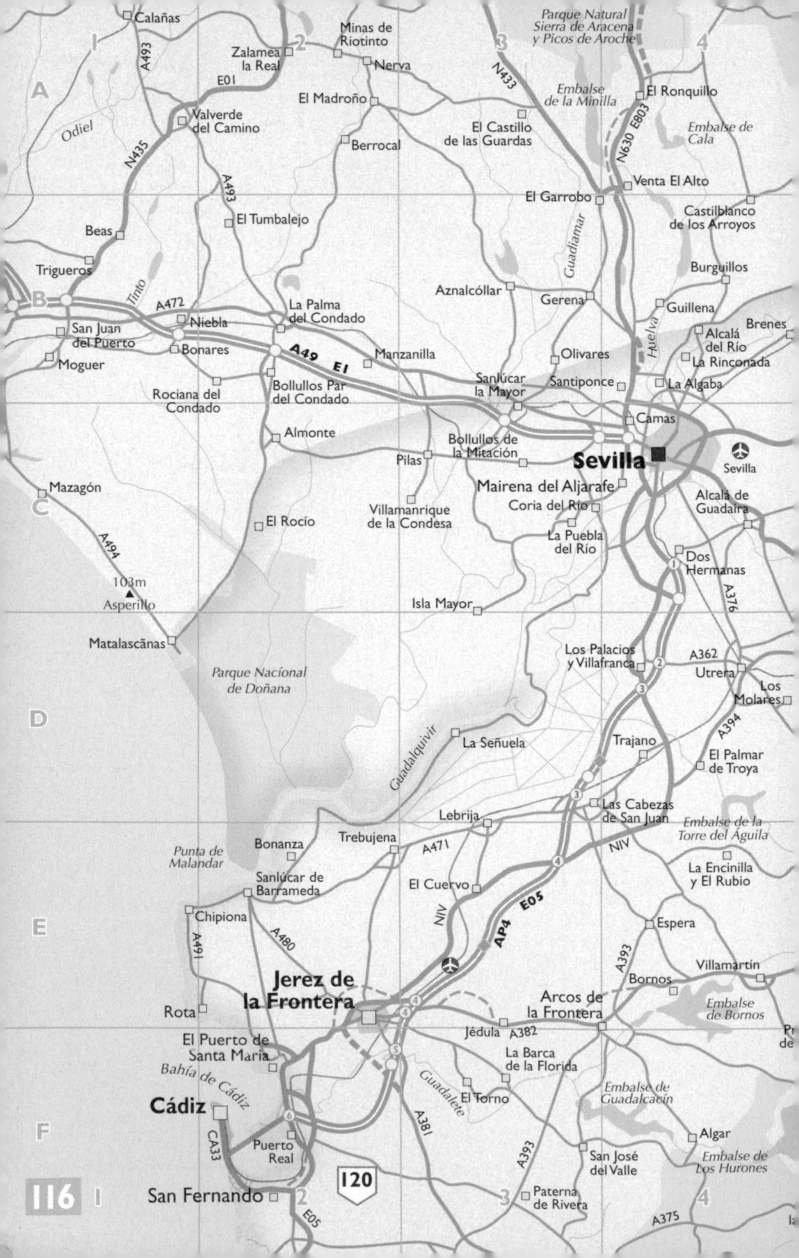
Calañas
Minas de Riotinto
Parque Natural Sierra de Aracena y Picos de Aroche
Zalamea la Real
Nerva
El Madroño
Valverde del Camino
Embalse de la Minilla
El Ronquillo
El Castillo de las Guardas
Embalse de Cala
Berrocal
Odiel
Venta El Alto
El Garrobo
Castilblanco de los Arroyos
El Tumbalejo
Beas
Guadiamar
Trigueros
Burguillos
Tinto
Aznalcóllar
Gerena
La Palma del Condado
Guillena
Niebla
San Juan del Puerto
Bonares
Moguer
Manzanilla
Brenes
Alcalá del Río
Olivares
La Rinconada
Huelva
Rociana del Condado
Bollullos Par del Condado
Sanlúcar la Mayor
Santiponce
La Algaba
Camas
Almonte
Bollullos de la Mitación
Pilas
Sevilla
Mairena del Aljarafe
Mazagón
Alcalá de Guadaira
Coria del Río
Villamanrique de la Condesa
El Rocío
La Puebla del Río
Dos Hermanas
103m
Asperillo
Isla Mayor
Matalascañas
Los Palacios y Villafranca
Utrera
Parque Nacional de Doñana
Los Molares
La Señuela
Trajano
El Palmar de Troya
Guadalquivir
Las Cabezas de San Juan
Lebrija
Embalse de la Torre del Águila
Trebujena
Punta de Malandar
Bonanza
La Encinilla y El Rubio
Sanlúcar de Barrameda
El Cuervo
Chipiona
Espera
Villamartín
Jerez de la Frontera
Bornos
Arcos de la Frontera
Embalse de Bornos
Rota
Jédula
El Puerto de Santa María
La Barca de la Florida
Bahía de Cádiz
Guadalete
El Torno
Embalse de Guadalcacín
Cádiz
Algar
Puerto Real
San José del Valle
Embalse de Los Hurones
San Fernando
Paterna de Rivera
A493
E01
N433
N630
E803
N435
A472
A49
E1
A494
A376
A362
A394
A471
NIV
E05
AP4
A480
A491
A393
A382
A381
CA33
A375
A
B
C
D
E
F
1
2
3
4
120

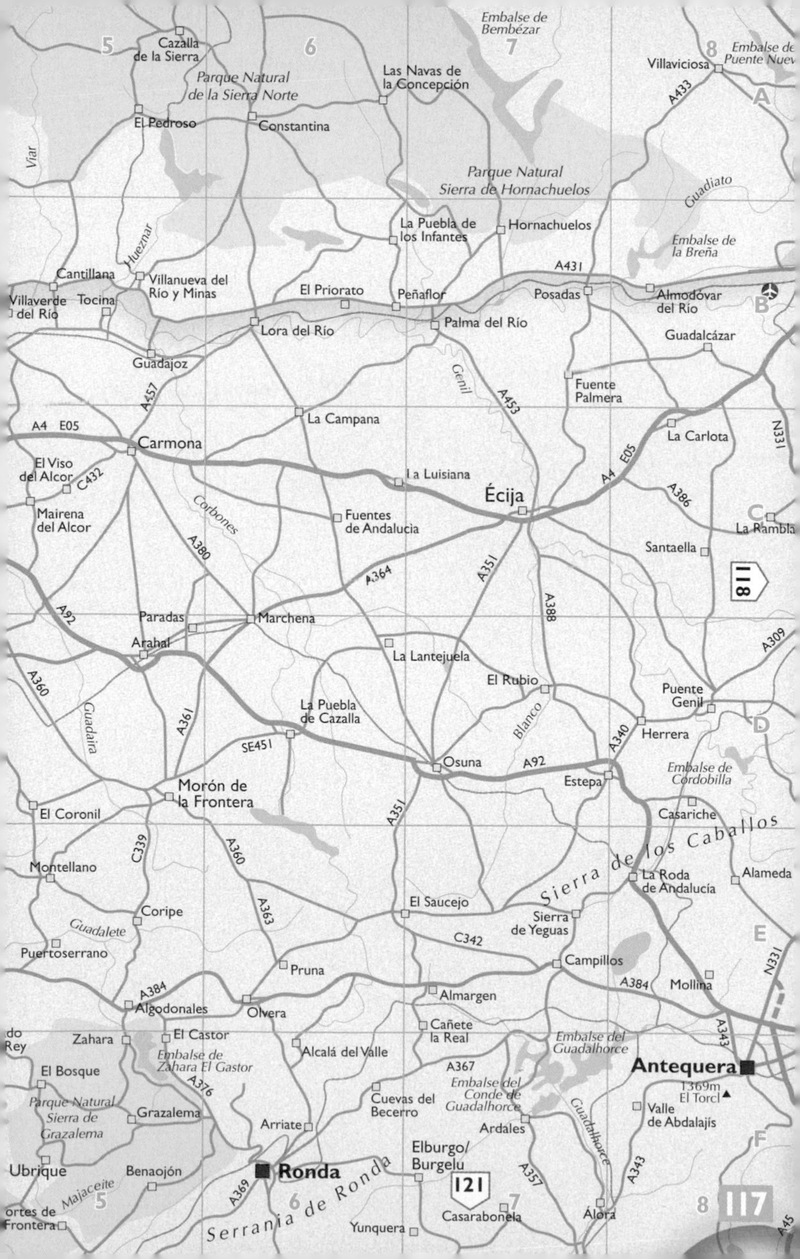
Cazalla de la Sierra
Parque Natural de la Sierra Norte
El Pedroso
Constantina
Las Navas de la Concepción
Embalse de Bembézar
Parque Natural Sierra de Hornachuelos
Villaviciosa
Embalse de Puente Nuevo
A433
Viar
Huesnar
Guadiato
La Puebla de los Infantes
Hornachuelos
Embalse de la Breña
A431
Cantillana
Villanueva del Río y Minas
Villaverde del Río
Tocina
El Priorato
Peñaflor
Posadas
Almodóvar del Río
Lora del Río
Palma del Río
Guadalcázar
Guadajoz
Genil
A453
Fuente Palmera
A457
La Campana
La Carlota
N331
A4 E05
Carmona
El Viso del Alcor
C432
La Luisiana
Écija
A386
Mairena del Alcor
Corbones
Fuentes de Andalucía
La Rambla
Santaella
A380
A364
A351
A388
118
A92
Paradas
Marchena
Arahal
A309
La Lantejuela
A360
El Rubio
Guadaira
Puente Genil
A361
La Puebla de Cazalla
Blanco
A340
Herrera
SE451
Osuna
A92
Estepa
Embalse de Cordobilla
Morón de la Frontera
El Coronil
A351
Casariche
Sierra de los Caballos
C339
A360
Montellano
La Roda de Andalucía
Alameda
A363
El Saucejo
Coripe
Sierra de Yeguas
Guadalete
C342
Puertoserrano
Campillos
N331
Pruna
A384
Mollina
A384
Almargen
Algodonales
Olvera
Cañete la Real
El Castor
Zahara
Embalse del Guadalhorce
A343
Embalse de Zahara El Gastor
Alcalá del Valle
El Bosque
A367
Antequera
A376
Embalse del Conde de Guadalhorce
1369m El Torcl
Parque Natural Sierra de Grazalema
Grazalema
Cuevas del Becerro
Valle de Abdalajís
Guadalhorce
Arriate
Ardales
Elburgo/Burgelu
Ubrique
Benaojón
Ronda
A357
A343
Majaceite
121
A369
Serranía de Ronda
Casarabonela
Álora
Yunquera
A45
5
6
7
8
A
B
C
D
E
F

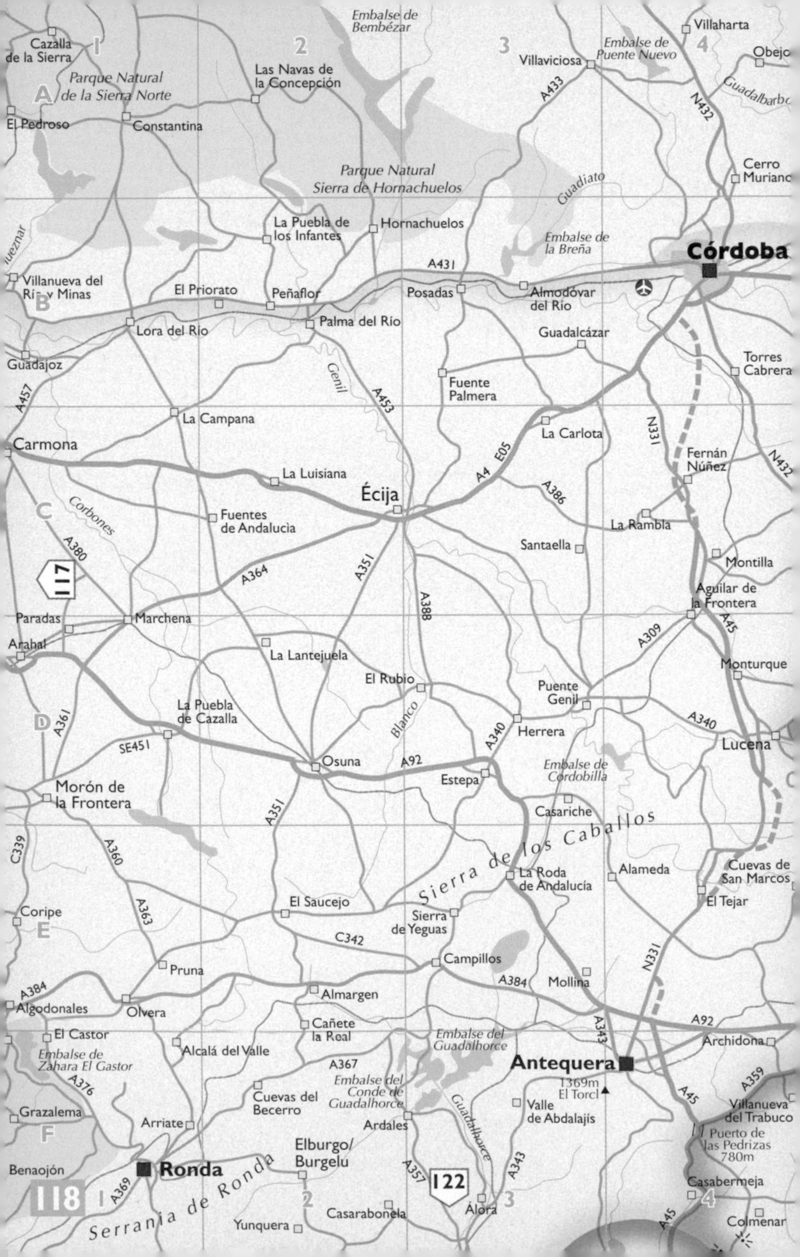

Cazalla de la Sierra
Parque Natural de la Sierra Norte
El Pedroso
Constantina
Las Navas de la Concepción
Embalse de Bembézar
Parque Natural Sierra de Hornachuelos
Villaviciosa
Embalse de Puente Nuevo
Villaharta
Obejo
Guadalbarbo
N432
A433
Guadiato
Cerro Muriano
La Puebla de los Infantes
Hornachuelos
Embalse de la Breña
Córdoba
A431
Villanueva del Río y Minas
El Priorato
Peñaflor
Posadas
Almodóvar del Río
Lora del Río
Palma del Río
Guadalcázar
Guadajoz
Genil
A453
Fuente Palmera
Torres Cabrera
A457
La Campana
La Carlota
N331
Carmona
Fernán Núñez
A4
E05
La Luisiana
Écija
A386
Corbones
Fuentes de Andalucía
La Rambla
A380
117
Santaella
Montilla
A364
A351
A388
Aguilar de la Frontera
Paradas
Marchena
A309
A45
Arahal
La Lantejuela
Monturque
El Rubio
Puente Genil
A361
La Puebla de Cazalla
Blanco
A340
Herrera
Lucena
SE451
Osuna
A92
Estepa
Embalse de Cordobilla
Morón de la Frontera
Casariche
Sierra de los Caballos
C339
A360
La Roda de Andalucía
Alameda
Cuevas de San Marcos
El Tejar
A363
El Saucejo
Sierra de Yeguas
Coripe
C342
Campillos
Pruna
A384
Mollina
A384
Algodonales
Olvera
Almargen
A343
A92
Cañete la Real
El Castor
Embalse del Guadalhorce
Archidona
Embalse de Zahara El Gastor
Alcalá del Valle
A367
Antequera
A376
Embalse del Conde de Guadalhorce
1369m El Torcl
A359
Cuevas del Becerro
Guadalhorce
Valle de Abdalajís
A45
Villanueva del Trabuco
Grazalema
Arriate
Ardales
Puerto de las Pedrizas 780m
Elburgo/ Burgelu
Benaojón
Ronda
Serranía de Ronda
A357
122
A343
Casabermeja
118
A369
Yunquera
Casarabonela
Álora
A45
Colmenar

5
6
7
8
A
B
C
D
E
F
Cardeña
Parque Natural Sierra de Andújar
Colonia Selladores
Parque Natural Sierra de Cardeña y Montoro
Yeguas
Embalse de Jandúla
N420
Adamuz
Embalse del Rumblar
Montoro
Marmolejo
Pedro Abad
El Carpio
Andújar
A4 E05
Bailén
Villa del Río
Lopera
Guadalquivir
Villanueva de la Reina
Bujalance
Arjona
A309
Porcuna
Mengíbar
A306
A321
Santiago de Calatrava
Fuerte del Rey
Villagordo
Espejo
A305
Guadalbullón
Castro del Río
A44
Izcar
Torredonjimeno
Torre del Compte
A316
Martos
Jaén
A316
Jimena
Nueva-Carteya
Baena
Embalse de Valdomojón
La Guardia de Jaén
Doña Mencía
Los Villares
Luque
Alcaudete
2167m
Zuheros
Cabra
E902
Guadajoz
N432
A333
Valdepeñas de Jaén
Carcabuey
Castillo de Locubín
Alcalá la Real
A340
Priego de Córdoba
Campillo de Arenas
Puerto de Carretero 1040m
Rute
Campotejar
Algarinejo
Iznájar
Puerto de Onitar 1040m
Embalse de Iznájar
Montefrío
Puerto del Zagrí 1080m
N432
Moclín
Píñar
Moreda
A335
Íllora
Iznalloz
Deifontes
A44
Huétor Tájar
A92
Pinos Puente
1931m
Loja
Fuente Vacqueros
Salar
Puerto de la Mora 1390m
Moraleda de Zafayona
Atarfe
A92
A335
Granada
Santa Fé
Castillo de Tajarja
Granada
Armilla
Monachil
A338
Güéjar Sierra
Ventas de Huelma
Cacín
Puerto del Suspiro del Moro 860m
La Zubia
123
A356
Ventas de Zefarraya
A395
Alhama de Granada
Sierra Nevada
Periana
E902

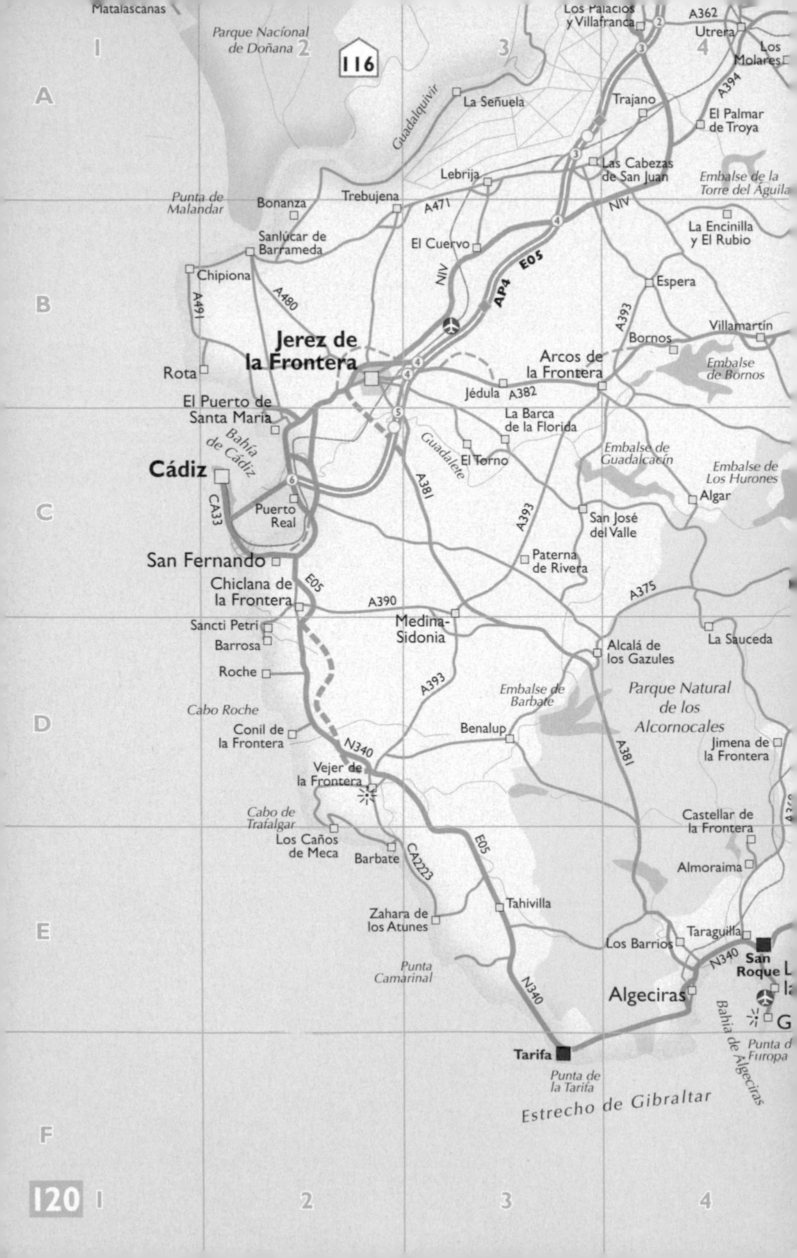
116
Matalascanas
Parque Nacíonal de Doñana
Los Palacios y Villafranca
A362
Utrera
Los Molares
Guadalquivir
La Señuela
Trajano
A394
El Palmar de Troya
Las Cabezas de San Juan
Lebrija
Embalse de la Torre del Águila
Punta de Malandar
Bonanza
Trebujena
A471
NIV
La Encinilla y El Rubio
Sanlúcar de Barrameda
El Cuervo
E05
AP4
Chipiona
A491
A480
Espera
A393
Villamartín
Bornos
Jerez de la Frontera
Arcos de la Frontera
Embalse de Bornos
Rota
Jédula
A382
El Puerto de Santa Maria
La Barca de la Florida
Bahía de Cádiz
Guadalete
El Torno
Embalse de Guadalcacín
Embalse de Los Hurones
Cádiz
A381
Algar
CA33
Puerto Real
San José del Valle
San Fernando
Paterna de Rivera
Chiclana de la Frontera
A390
A375
Medina-Sidonia
Sancti Petri
Barrosa
Alcalá de los Gazules
La Sauceda
Roche
Embalse de Barbate
Parque Natural de los Alcornocales
Cabo Roche
Conil de la Frontera
Benalup
Jimena de la Frontera
N340
Vejer de la Frontera
Cabo de Trafalgar
Los Caños de Meca
Barbate
CA2223
Castellar de la Frontera
Almoraima
Tahivilla
Zahara de los Atunes
Los Barrios
Taraguilla
San Roque
Punta Camarinal
Algeciras
Bahía de Algeciras
Tarifa
Punta de Europa
Punta de la Tarifa
Estrecho de Gibraltar
A B C D E F
1 2 3 4

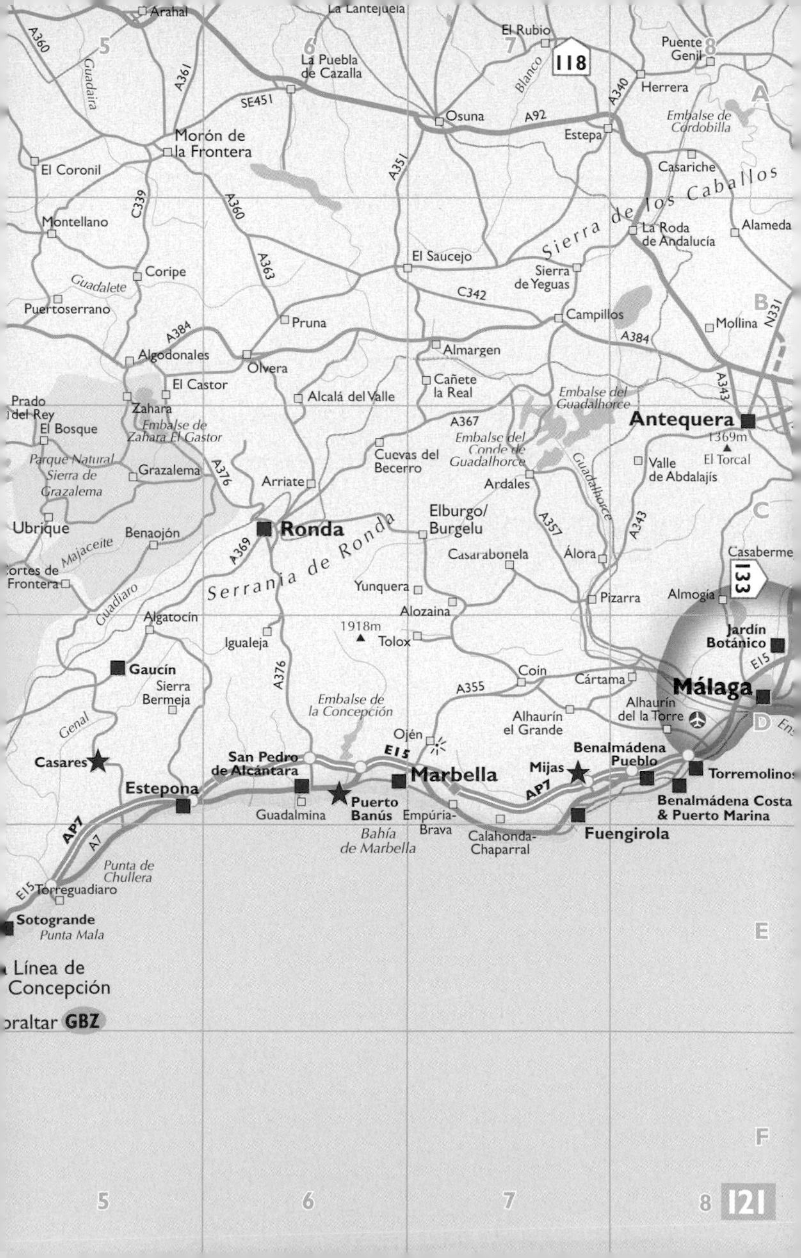
Arahal
La Lantejuela
El Rubio
118
Puente Genil
A360
5
6
7
8
Guadaira
A361
La Puebla de Cazalla
Blanco
A340
Herrera
A
SE451
Osuna
A92
Embalse de Cordobilla
Estepa
Morón de la Frontera
El Coronil
A351
Casariche
A360
Sierra de los Caballos
C339
Montellano
La Roda de Andalucía
Alameda
A363
El Saucejo
Coripe
Guadalete
Sierra de Yeguas
C342
Puertoserrano
B
N331
Campillos
Pruna
Mollina
A384
A384
Almargen
Algodonales
Olvera
Cañete la Real
El Castor
A343
Alcalá del Valle
Embalse del Guadalhorce
Prado del Rey
Zahara
A367
Antequera
El Bosque
Embalse de Zahara El Gastor
1369m
Embalse del Conde de Guadalhorce
El Torcal
Cuevas del Becerro
Parque Natural Sierra de Grazalema
Grazalema
Valle de Abdalajís
A376
Arriate
Ardales
Guadalhorce
C
Elburgo/ Burgelu
Ubrique
Ronda
A357
A343
Benaojón
Majaceite
A369
Serrania de Ronda
Casarabonela
Álora
Casaberme
Cortes de Frontera
133
Yunquera
Pizarra
Almogía
Guadiaro
Alozaina
Algatocín
1918m
Jardín Botánico
Igualeja
Tolox
E15
Gaucín
Coín
A376
Cártama
Sierra Bermeja
A355
Málaga
Embalse de la Concepción
Alhaurín del la Torre
Genal
Alhaurín el Grande
D
Ojén
Benalmádena Pueblo
E15
Casares
San Pedro de Alcántara
Mijas
Marbella
Torremolinos
Estepona
AP7
Puerto Banús
Benalmádena Costa & Puerto Marina
Guadalmina
Empúria-Brava
AP7
Fuengirola
A7
Bahía de Marbella
Calahonda-Chaparral
Punta de Chullera
E15
Torreguadiaro
Sotogrande
Punta Mala
E
Línea de Concepción
GBZ
F
5
6
7
8

Arahal
La Lantejuela
El Rubio
118
Monturque
Puente Genil
La Puebla de Cazalla
Blanco
A361
SE451
Osuna
A92
A340
Herrera
A340
Lucena
Embalse de Cordobilla
Morón de la Frontera
Estepa
Casariche
A351
C339
A360
Sierra de los Caballos
La Roda de Andalucía
Alameda
Cuevas de San Marcos
El Tejar
El Saucejo
Sierra de Yeguas
A363
Coripe
C342
N331
Campillos
Pruna
Mollina
A384
A384
Algodonales
Almargen
Olvera
A92
El Castor
Cañete la Real
A343
Alcalá del Valle
Zahara
Embalse del Guadalhorce
Archidona
Embalse de Zahara El Gastor
A367
Antequera
Embalse del Conde de Guadalhorce
1369m
A45
A359
Cuevas del Becerro
El Torcal
Valle de Abdalajís
Guadalhorce
Villanueva del Trabuco
Grazalema
A376
Ardales
Arriate
Puerto de las Pedrizas 780m
Elburgo/ Burgelu
Ronda
A357
A343
Benaojón
Serrania de Ronda
Casarabonela
Álora
Casabermeja
A369
121
Colmenar
Yunquera
Pizarra
Almogía
Alozaina
Algatocín
1918m
Tolox
Jardín Botánico
A45
Puerto del León 960m
Igualeja
E15
Gaucín
Coín
Cártama
Sierra Bermeja
A376
A355
Málaga
Embalse de la Concepción
Alhaurín del la Torre
Alhaurín el Grande
El Palo
La Cala del Moral
Ojén
Ensenada de Málaga
E15
San Pedro de Alcántara
Benalmádena Pueblo
Mijas
Rincón de la V
Marbella
Torremolinos
Estepona
AP7
Guadalmina
Puerto Banús
Empúria-Brava
Benalmádena Costa & Puerto Marina
Bahía de Marbella
Calahonda-Chaparral
Fuengirola
1
2
3
4
A
B
C
D
E
F

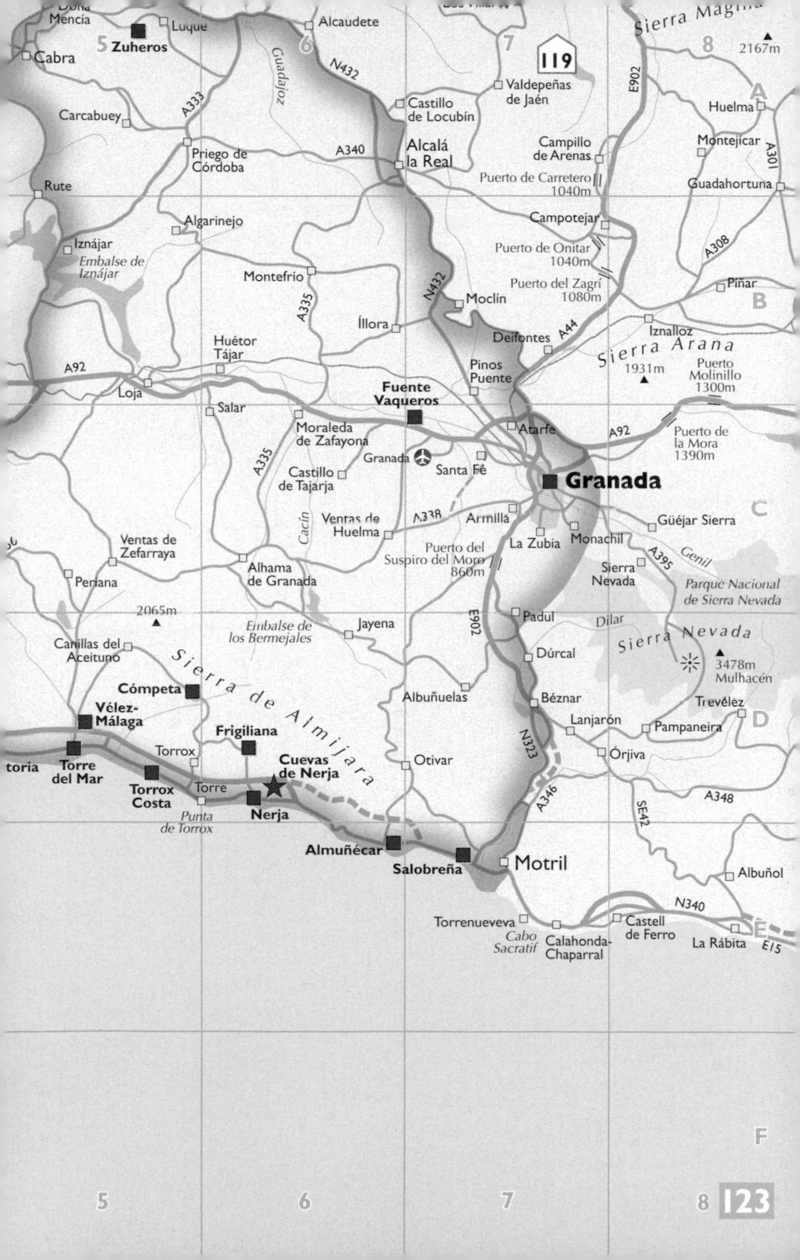

Mencía
Zuheros
Luque
Alcaudete
Cabra
119
Sierra Mágina
2167m
Guadajoz
N432
A333
Valdepeñas de Jaén
Carcabuey
Castillo de Locubín
E902
Huelma
A340
Alcalá la Real
Campillo de Arenas
Montejícar
A301
Priego de Córdoba
Puerto de Carretero 1040m
Guadahortuna
Rute
Campotejar
Algarinejo
Iznájar
Embalse de Iznájar
Puerto de Onitar 1040m
A308
Montefrío
N432
Puerto del Zagrí 1080m
Piñar
A335
Moclín
Íllora
A44
Deifontes
Iznalloz
Sierra Arana
Huétor Tájar
Pinos Puente
1931m
Puerto Molinillo 1300m
A92
Loja
Fuente Vaqueros
Salar
Moraleda de Zafayona
Atarfe
A92
Puerto de la Mora 1390m
Granada
A335
Santa Fé
Castillo de Tajarja
Granada
Cacín
Ventas de Huelma
A338
Armilla
Güéjar Sierra
La Zubia
Monachil
Ventas de Zefarraya
Puerto del Suspiro del Moro 860m
A395
Genil
Periana
Alhama de Granada
Sierra Nevada
Parque Nacional de Sierra Nevada
2065m
E902
Padul
Dilar
Embalse de los Bermejales
Jayena
Sierra Nevada
Canillas del Aceituno
Dúrcal
3478m Mulhacén
Sierra de Almijara
Cómpeta
Albuñuelas
Béznar
Trevélez
Vélez-Málaga
N323
Lanjarón
Pampaneira
Frigiliana
Torrox
Órjiva
toria
Torre del Mar
Cuevas de Nerja
Otivar
Torrox Costa
Torre
A346
A348
SE42
Punta de Torrox
Nerja
Almuñécar
Salobreña
Motril
Albuñol
N340
Torrenueveva
Cabo Sacratif
Calahonda-Chaparral
Castell de Ferro
La Rábita
E15

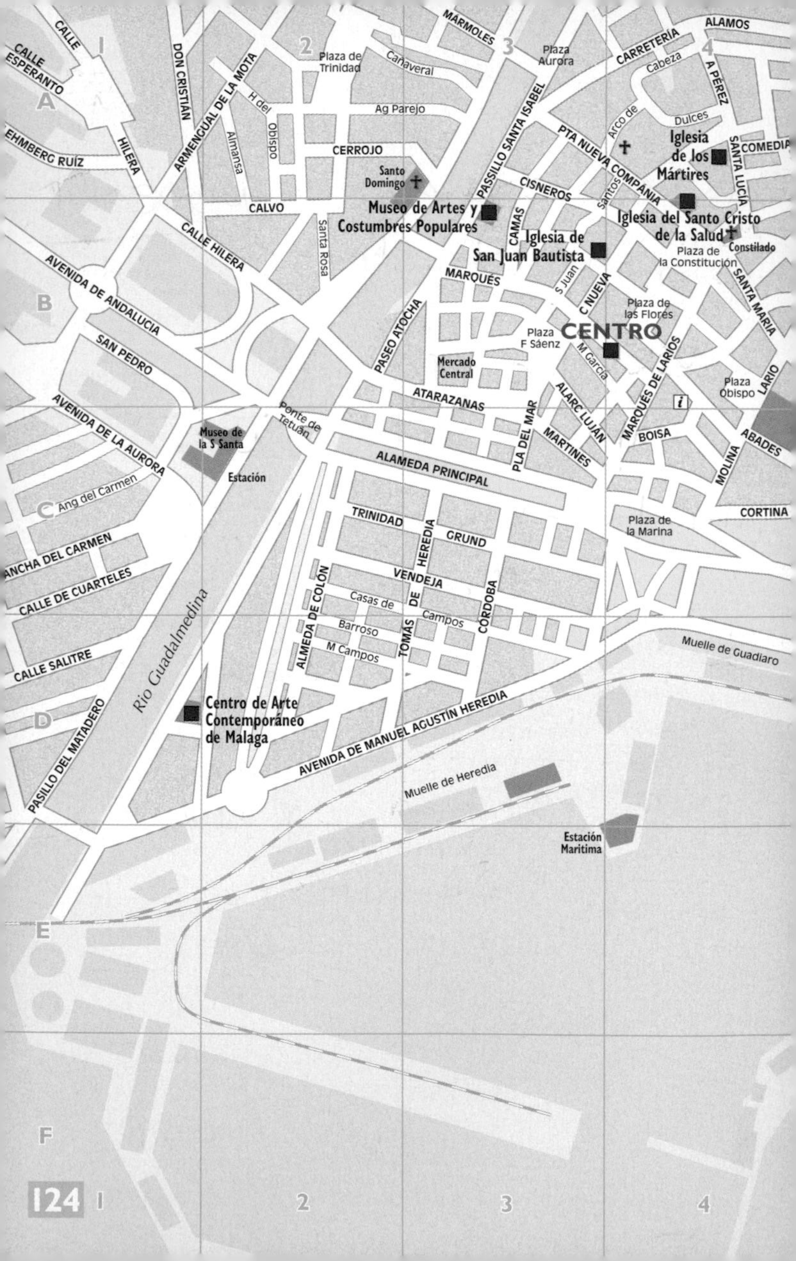

CALLE
CALLE ESPERANTO
EHMBERG RUÍZ
HILERA
DON CRISTIÁN
ARMENGUAL DE LA MOTA
H del
Obispo
Almansa
Plaza de Trinidad
Cañaveral
Ag Parejo
CERROJO
MARMOLES
Plaza Aurora
CARRETERÍA
ALAMOS
Cabeza
A PÉREZ
Arco de
Dulces
Iglesia de los Mártires
COMEDIA
SANTA LUCÍA
PASILLO SANTA ISABEL
PTA NUEVA COMPAÑÍA
Santos
CISNEROS
Santo Domingo
CALVO
Museo de Artes y Costumbres Populares
CAMAS
Iglesia del Santo Cristo de la Salud
Constilado
Plaza de la Constitución
Iglesia de San Juan Bautista
Santa Rosa
CALLE HILERA
MARQUÉS
S Juan
C NUEVA
SANTA MARÍA
AVENIDA DE ANDALUCÍA
Plaza de las Flores
SAN PEDRO
PASEO ATOCHA
Plaza F Sáenz
CENTRO
M García
MARQUÉS DE LARIOS
Mercado Central
LARIO
Plaza Obispo
ATARAZANAS
ALARC LUJÁN
AVENIDA DE LA AURORA
Ponte de Tetuán
PLA DEL MAR
MARTINES
BOISA
ABADES
Museo de la S Santa
ALAMEDA PRINCIPAL
MOLINA
Estación
Ang del Carmen
CORTINA
TRINIDAD
HEREDIA
GRUND
Plaza de la Marina
ANCHA DEL CARMEN
VENDEJA
CALLE DE CUARTELES
ALMEDA DE COLÓN
Casas de
DE
Campos
CÓRDOBA
Barroso
TOMÁS
M Campos
Muelle de Guadiaro
Rio Guadalmedina
CALLE SALITRE
Centro de Arte Contemporáneo de Malaga
PASILLO DEL MATADERO
AVENIDA DE MANUEL AGUSTÍN HEREDIA
Muelle de Heredia
Estación Maritima
1
2
3
4
A
B
C
D
E
F

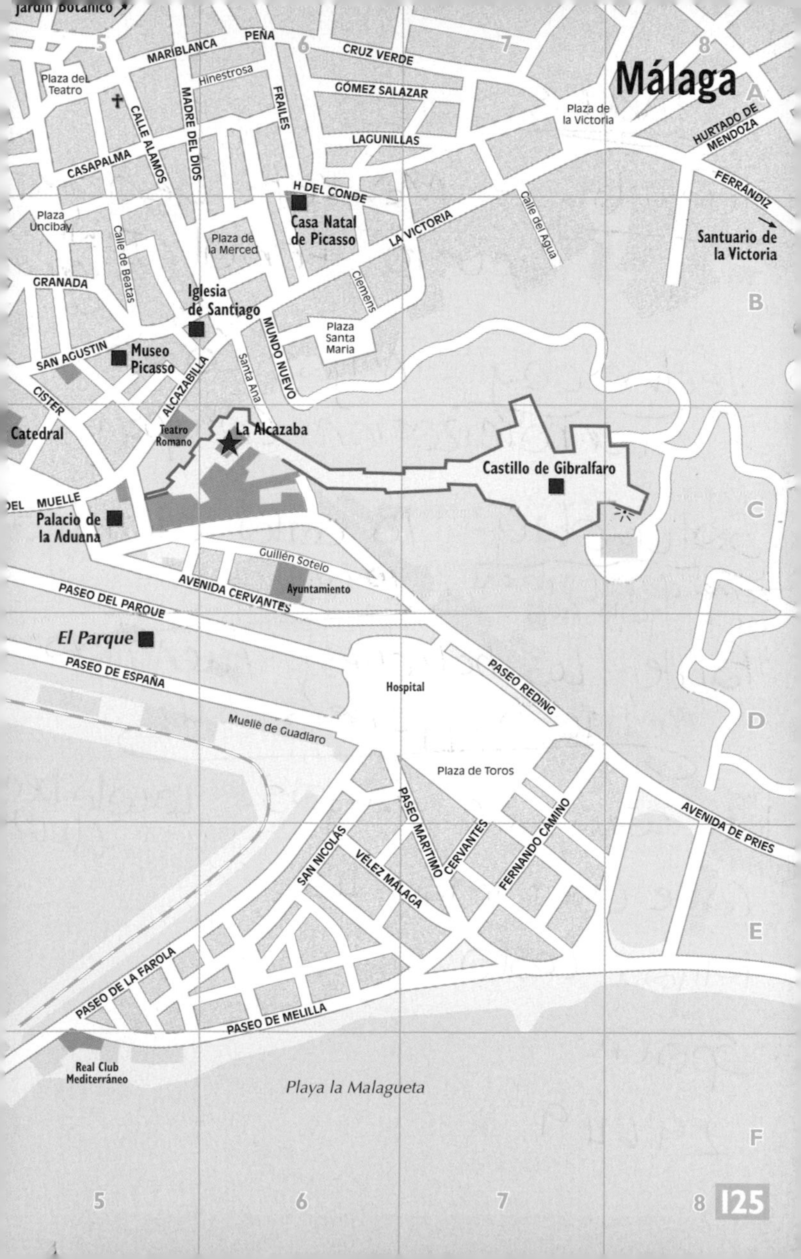

Jardín Botánico
Málaga
MARIBLANCA
PEÑA
CRUZ VERDE
Plaza del Teatro
Hinestrosa
GÓMEZ SALAZAR
CALLE ALAMOS
MADRE DEL DIOS
FRAILES
Plaza de la Victoria
HURTADO DE MENDOZA
LAGUNILLAS
CASAPALMA
H DEL CONDE
FERRANDIZ
Plaza Uncibay
Calle de Beatas
Plaza de la Merced
Casa Natal de Picasso
LA VICTORIA
Calle del Agua
Santuario de la Victoria
GRANADA
Iglesia de Santiago
Clemens
MUNDO NUEVO
Plaza Santa Maria
SAN AGUSTIN
Museo Picasso
ALCAZABILLA
Santa Ana
CISTER
La Alcazaba
Teatro Romano
Catedral
Castillo de Gibralfaro
DEL MUELLE
Palacio de la Aduana
Guillén Sotelo
AVENIDA CERVANTES
Ayuntamiento
PASEO DEL PARQUE
El Parque
PASEO DE ESPAÑA
Hospital
PASEO REDING
Muelle de Guadiaro
Plaza de Toros
PASEO MARITIMO
CERVANTES
FERNANDO CAMINO
AVENIDA DE PRIES
SAN NICOLÁS
VÉLEZ MÁLAGA
PASEO DE LA FAROLA
PASEO DE MELILLA
Real Club Mediterráneo
Playa la Malagueta
5
6
7
8
A
B
C
D
E
F

MARKETS Notes

Tuesday - Market Fuengirola
Recinto Ferial (Town Fairground)

Wednesday - Mijas Costa
Urbanization Calypso

Saturday - la cala di Mijas
corner of road leading up to Lacala Golf. 10-2pm

Failte Los boliches Fuengirola.
Celtic Supporters Club.

La cala de mijas Lacala beach club

Calle Cartama 43

Mijas Costa

Spain

29649.